INVITATION TO THE
GARDEN

INVITATION TO THE
GARDEN

A LITERARY AND PHOTOGRAPHIC CELEBRATION

EDITED BY FERRIS COOK

PHOTOGRAPHS BY

PING AMRANAND

KEN DRUSE

RICHARD FELBER

MICK HALES

HARRY HARALAMBOU

PETER C. JONES

PETER MARGONELLI

HUGH PALMER

CURTICE TAYLOR

STEWART, TABORI & CHANG

NEW YORK

Published in 1992 by
Stewart, Tabori & Chang, Inc.
575 Broadway, New York, New York 10012

Library of Congress Cataloging-in-Publication Data
Invitation to the garden : a literary and photographic celebration /
    edited by Ferris Cook ; photographs by Ping Amranand . . . [et al.].
        p.   cm.
    Includes index.
    ISBN 1-55670-182-9
    1. Gardens—Pictorial works. 2. Gardens—Literary collections.
I. Cook, Ferris.   II. Amranand, Ping.
SB450.98.I58   1992
712—dc20   92-1512
                                                               CIP

Distributed in the U.S. by Workman Publishing,
708 Broadway, New York, New York 10003
Distributed in Canada by Canadian Manda Group,
P.O. Box 920 Station U, Toronto, Ontario M8Z 5P9

Printed in Japan
10 9 8 7 6 5 4 3 2 1

PAGE 1: HUGH PALMER, *Cotoneaster horizontalis* at Epwell Mill,
Oxfordshire, England

PAGE 2: HUGH PALMER, Peonies, honeysuckle, and pineapple broom
(*Cytisus Battandieri*) at Cornwell Manor, Oxfordshire, England

PAGES 6–7: PING AMRANAND, Tulip garden, Charlottesville, Virginia

PAGE 8, TOP: HUGH PALMER, Lily-flowered tulips and forget-me-nots at
Clare College, Cambridge, England; BOTTOM: PETER C. JONES,
Clematis × *Jackmanii*, Coastal Rhode Island

PAGE 9, TOP: KEN DRUSE, Shore juniper, fountain grass (*Pennisetum
alopecuroides*), sourwood (*Oxydendrum arboreum*), and *Sedum*
'Autumn Joy', Long Island, New York; BOTTOM: HUGH PALMER,
Willows including *Salix daphnoides* and colored forms of *Salix alba*
at Dower House in Boughton, Northamptonshire, England

PAGES 16–17: MICK HALES, Pansies and *Tulipa* 'Apricot Beauty', 'Mary
Poppins', and 'Black Swan', Philadelphia, Pennsylvania

PAGES 72–73: MICK HALES, Tomatoes, Hereford, England

PAGES 158–159: RICHARD FELBER, Innisfree Garden, Millbrook,
New York

PAGES 194–195: PING AMRANAND, Pebble Garden at Dumbarton Oaks,
Washington, D.C.

this is the garden: colours come and go,
frail azures fluttering from night's outer wing
strong silent greens serenely lingering,
absolute lights like baths of golden snow.
This is the garden: pursed lips do blow
upon cool flutes within wide glooms, and sing
(of harps celestial to the quivering string)
invisible faces hauntingly and slow.

This is the garden.   Time shall surely reap
and on Death's blade lie many a flower curled,
in other lands where other songs be sung;
yet stand They here enraptured, as among
the slow deep trees perpetual of sleep
some silver-fingered fountain steals the world.

e.e. cummings

ACKNOWLEDGMENTS

I would like to thank the many people who have been involved in the production of *Invitation to the Garden.* The idea of a book combining poetry, short stories, and essays came from Brian Hotchkiss, formerly an editor at Stewart, Tabori & Chang, while my sister, Sarah Longacre, the photo editor, proposed featuring the work of photographers who have been associated with the publisher. I am indebted to the photographers for their beautiful work, patience, and cooperation.

Sarah Longacre also handled the gathering and sorting of thousands of pictures, with help from Rebecca Williams, Jose Pouso, and Jeremiah Bogert. Julie Rauer arrived at the deceptively simple design, and Ruth Diamond made it possible for us to meet our deadlines.

To my friend and editor Jennie McGregor Bernard I owe special thanks. Not only did she handle all of the pieces of the puzzle, but she did so with good humor. Both Jennie and her assistant Miki Porta read carefully through the texts and worried with me over details. Thanks also to Susannah Levy for her care in following up with the paperwork, and to my husband Ken Krabbenhoft, who has introduced me to many writers, including Fernando Pessoa and Clarice Lispector. Without his influence this book would have been much narrower in scope.

CONTENTS

AUTUMN

158

WINTER

194

FOREWORD

Like so many other gardeners separated from their gardens by darkness, miles, or inclement weather, I love to read about other gardens when I can't be in mine. While plant materials differ between regions and hemispheres, the love of growing things is universal. More than simply a stage for perennials and bulbs, fragrance and color, gardens have provided a variety of inspiration for writers.

The attempt to capture an experience as fleeting as the first signs of spring can be as close as the following poem by Prentiss Moore:

POEM

one sees the budding of
trees it seems always
two or three days after it
begins, like awakening
from a sound one did not
actually hear

Joseph Wood Krutch writes about a similar experience in *The Twelve Seasons* (1949) when he laments his inability to see a blade of grass first emerge: "Who can say that he ever saw a blade of grass come up out of the ground, much less that he ever saw one of the spears which survived the winter turn green? These things do nevertheless happen, and suddenly one is aware that they have happened."

It's impossible to define a season by a specific month that would be common to all of us.

So gradually do the seasons change that, as Miss Henrietta Wilson writes from Scotland in *The Chronicles of a Garden,* 1864, "we scarcely know whether to class the month of May as the last of the spring months or the first of those of summer." When I notice the grass turn green in New York it's probably April, but in California it may be November. The sequence of bloom, however, is apt to be similar from one place to another, and lends continuity to the gardener's year. But when does the garden year begin?

For the fortunate gardeners who live beside their gardens, the garden is in a constant state of beginning. For those of us who work in one place and garden in another, there are definite beginnings and endings in the garden year. In my case, my husband, son and I arrive in the garden after the exile of an artificial year in Manhattan imposed by the school year. This is the first of five irregular periods in my garden in upstate New York.

In these first weeks extending into mid-July, I spend the most hours in the garden. Aside from weeding the garden, I spend a lot of time planting and nursing the seedlings I've started indoors in early spring. August is the second season of my garden year: it's hot and dry, and I avoid the yard. I put away my tools and ignore the weeds. No other time of year is so discouraging for me. Even February beckons some reflection. So, it is only after a change of heart and weather that I begin again in September. In this, my third season, I move plants and make a final weeding. The weather cools, and some rain falls. The garden is reopened. The asters and perennial bachelor's buttons with their profuse color invite inspection, and the chrysanthemums and snakeroots promise the same from an abundance of buds. My contacts with other gardeners are renewed as many of the plants need dividing, moving, discarding, or trading. The scattering of seeds and rearrangement of plants brings an unknown outcome, and the anticipation of the spring garden begins.

In winter, which often sets in on Thanksgiving weekend, the catalogs lure me to new schemes. I re-draw the plans of the garden in my notebook and wait, while watching my scarred hands heal. The fifth and last season comes in March, when the first patches of color show in my garden, and there's nothing to do yet but look. It's my favorite time, and I hastily place shrub and plant orders, tend seedlings on my windowsills, and am caught up in expectations all out of proportion to the efforts I've made. The bulbs appear in my garden, and the color and fragrance increase weekly. When the soil is warmer and dry enough to dig, I spend every weekend, dawn to dusk, working in the garden. By the time I arrive for summer vacation, the garden is in full bloom.

Gardeners tend to imagine different beginnings for their gardens. Louise Shelton in *The Seasons in a Flower Garden* (1906) begins a section on "The Garden Record" by dating the beginning to September. "If you ask why I begin this record of the flower seasons at the end of summer, I will tell you that this is the month [September] of spring-hopes in the gardener's dreamland, the time to plan for the next far away birth-time of flowers, when gardens burst forth in blossom and perfume after the long, deep sleep. This is also resting-time in the harvest sunshine, a breathing space when the summer's work is done and we revel in the fruits of our labor. . . . It is mid-September before we need cease our all-day idling in the garden." Elizabeth Lawrence also sees the garden's true beginning in the autumn. In her book *Gardens in Winter* (1961) she observes: "There are two awakenings in the garden: one in spring, and one in autumn. But it is in autumn, when frost puts an end to the old year's bloom, that the garden year really begins; for then the pointed buds of the winter-flowering bulbs are breaking through the ground, and the buds of the wintersweet are beginning to swell. Soon afterward, stems of the Christmas-roses hump up, pulling the buds to the light, and when spring comes it finds winter flowers still in bloom."

I must admit that cooler weather, beautiful as it is, feels to me more like a second wind than the first leg of a race. I haven't always the perserverance to do all I can, knowing the finish line is near. The frost is coming. There aren't many dates in the gardening year as dramatic as the fall frost. Richardson Wright describes the Black Frost in *The Gardener's Bed-Book* (1939): "Other frosts—White Frosts—have come and gone with their petty destructions. The mercury has danced up and down its tube like a coloratura soprano running her scales. We've had brisk days and days languorously warm. What remains of the garden is very precious because it has so short a time to live. We hope for a reprieve all the while, knowing that the Tsar of Winter must visit his wrath eventually. . . . And then one night it comes—sweeps down from the north silently on a still night. We awake to find the garden blackened. The miserable cadavers of our flowers hang with bowed head on the scaffold of Winter." By the late fall, in a garden hit hard by a deep freeze, I feel the joy of seeing the shape of the garden anew. In early November, when most of the leaves have fallen, I can see the structure, see the year's growth of the young evergreens I've been raising for eventual screening. They have been growing inconspicuously in the perennial beds. At this season, they lend little shape to the garden since they're still so small. And by winter, when it's possible to tramp over the frozen ground and stand in the impenetrable patches of the summer garden, such as the daylily bed, I envision new solutions.

Each season in the garden prompts different action, and brings its own urgency. For various reasons, some gardeners think of winter, rather than summer or fall, as the start of the garden year. But for me it's the thing we are anticipating, the tender new and perfect growth of the spring flowers, that seems like the signpost for the new year. In *The Countryman's Year*

(1936), for instance, David Grayson agrees, "I had some doubt, in beginning this book, where it would be best to break into the magic circle of the seasons, whether at the conventional entrance, in January, or at the first faint intimacies of the awakening of spring. In the old calendars the New Year began with the vernal equinox in March, according to the logic of the sun and the moon and the stars, but restless human beings will be forever trying to vote their own way; and when the Gregorian calendar was adopted in America in the year 1752 New Year's Day was changed from March 25 to January 1." So, he chooses for himself, and begins his book on April 1st.

For this book, I have followed his example and have chosen spring, when the ground is soggy, and all I dare do is look. But it's not so easy to fix a date. While garden calendars date the season to the spring equinox, the 21st of the month, Alfred Simson in *Garden Mosaics* (1903) begins his year on March 7th: "In my garden I wish to consider that spring set in on the 7th of March. . . . On the 7th and the few days which have elapsed since, the garden, in comparison with winter, has looked quite gay with its long fringes and clumps of crocuses, snowdrops, violets, and hepaticas in full bloom, and it is quite clear the winter slumber is over, and the hope sown in autumn has developed into full-fledged expectation. The first primroses, chionodoxas, and polyanthus are also in flower, whilst the rhododendrons, azaleas, cherries, the older anemones, daffodils, and other trees and bulbs have pushed out their healthy flower-buds. Many of the irises, hyacinths, tulips, narcissus, delphiniums, campanulas, sweet-williams, Canterbury bells, and pansies show vigorous new growth; and the leaf-buds have swollen and are opening on roses, honeysuckle, Billy Button, clematis, lilacs, and others. . . . If all this, when I am now writing on the 10th of March, is not stronger evidence than the bald and unsupported statement that 'spring commences' on the 21st of March, may some of my buds be cut off by late frosts—as they probably will be." Looking at my garden records, I find scant blossoms of interest in March. Just "a few clumps of snowdrops by the barn" always within a couple of days of March 1st, and brief remarks on crocuses. No botanical names, and no observations of fat buds.

Luckily I don't need a specific date for this book. Spring is a general idea, and its anticipation can be stimulated at odd times of the year. As I write, I am looking out of my north-facing windows in New York City. It is mid-afternoon on a cold February day, but it's the only time of year when I get direct sunlight in my window. It's true that it's reflected light, but it reminds me that spring's just around the corner.

FERRIS COOK
NEW YORK CITY
FEBRUARY 1992

SPRING

DOWN THE GARDEN PATH

BEVERLEY NICHOLS

Whenever I arrive in my garden, I Make the Tour. Is this a personal idiosyncrasy, or do all good gardeners do it? It would be interesting to know. By Making the Tour, I mean only that I step from the front window, turn to the right, and make an infinitely detailed examination of every foot of ground, every shrub and tree, walking always over an appointed course.

There are certain very definite rules to be observed when you are Making the Tour. The chief rule is that you must never take anything out of its order. You may be longing to see if a crocus has come out in the orchard, but it is strictly forbidden to look before you have inspected all the various beds, bushes, and trees that lead up to the orchard.

You must not look at the bed ahead before you have finished with the bed immediately in front of you. You may see, out of the corner of your eye, a gleam of strange and unsuspected scarlet in the next bed but one, but you must steel yourself against rushing to this exciting blaze, and you must stare with cool eyes at the earth in front, which is apparently blank, until you have made certain that it is not hiding anything. Otherwise, you will find that you rush wildly round the garden, discover one or two sensational events, and then decide that nothing else has happened. Which means that you miss all the thrill of tiny shoots, the first lifting of the lids of the wall-flowers, the first precious gold of the witch-hazel, the early spear of the snowdrop. Which recalls one of the loveliest conceits in English poetry, Coventry Patmore's line about the snowdrop:

"And hails far summer with a lifted spear!"

It would require at least sixteen thick volumes bound in half calf, with bevelled edges, to contain a full account of a typical tour round any garden. There is so much history in every foot of soil.

—FROM *DOWN THE GARDEN PATH*

PING
AMRANAND

Forsythia Hill at Dumbarton Oaks
Washington, D.C.

PETER
MARGONELLI

Candelabra primulas with
Osmunda cinnamomea and
Symplocarpus foetidus
Southwestern Connecticut

THE PRIMROSE

JOHN DONNE

Upon this Primrose hill,
Where, if Heav'n would distill
A shourer of raine, each severall drop might goe
To his owne primrose, and grow Manna so;
And where their forme, and their infinitie
Make a terrestriall Galaxie,
As the small starres doe in the skie:
I walke to finde a true Love; and I see
That 'tis not a mere woman, that is shee,
But must, or more, or lesse than woman bee.

Yet know I not, which flower
I wish; a sixe, or foure;
For should my true-Love lesse then woman bee,
She were scarce any thing; and then, should she
Be more then woman, shee would get above
All thought of sexe, and thinke to move
My heart to study' her, and not to love;
Both these were monsters; Since there must reside
Falshood in woman, I could more abide,
She were by art, then Nature falsify'd.

Live Primrose, then, and thrive
With thy true number five;
And women, whom this flower doth represent,
With this mysterious number be content;
Ten is the farthest number; if halfe ten
Belonge unto each woman, then
Each woman may take halfe us men,
Or if this will not serve their turne, Since all
Numbers are odde or even, and they fall
First into this five, women may take us all.

One day when the bluebells were in bloom I wrote the following. I do not think I have ever seen anything more beautiful than the bluebell I have been looking at. I know the beauty of our Lord by it. It is strength and grace, like an ash. The head is strongly drawn over and arched down like a cutwater. The lines of the bells strike and overlie this, rayed but not symmetrically, some lie parallel. They look steely against paper, the shades lying between the bells and behind the cockled petal-ends and nursing up the precision of their distinctness, the petal-ends themselves being delicately lit. Then there is the straightness of the trumpets in the bells softened by the slight entasis and the square splay of the mouth.

—FROM DIARY ENTRY OF 1870

HUGH
PALMER

Bluebells and lime trees at
Morton House
Edinburgh, Scotland

THE SECRET GARDEN

FRANCES HODGSON BURNETT

She put her hands under the leaves and began to pull and push them aside. Thick as the ivy hung, it nearly all was a loose and swinging curtain, though some had crept over wood and iron. Mary's heart began to thump and her hands to shake a little in her delight and excitement. The robin kept singing and twittering away and tilting his head on one side, as if he were as excited as she was. What was this under her hands which was square and made of iron and which her fingers found a hole in?

It was the lock of the door which had been closed ten years, and she put her hand in her pocket, drew out the key, and found it fitted the keyhole. She put the key in and turned it. It took two hands to do it, but it did turn.

And then she took a long breath and looked behind her up the long walk to see if anyone was coming. No one was coming. No one ever did come, it seemed, and she took another long breath, because she could not help it, and she held back the swinging curtain of ivy and pushed back the door which opened slowly—slowly.

Then she slipped through it, and shut it behind her, and stood with her back against it, looking about her and breathing quite fast with excitement, and wonder, and delight.

She was standing *inside* the secret garden.

It was the sweetest, most mysterious-looking place anyone could imagine. The high walls which shut it in were covered with the leafless stems of climbing roses, which were so thick that they were matted together. Mary Lennox knew they were roses because she had seen a great many roses in India. All the ground was covered with grass of a wintry brown, and out of it grew clumps of bushes which were surely rose-bushes if they were alive. There were numbers of standard roses which had so spread their branches that they were like little trees. There were other trees in the garden, and one of the things which made the place look strangest and loveliest was that climbing roses had run all over them and swung down long tendrils which made light swaying curtains, and here and there they had caught at each other or at a far-reaching branch and had crept from one tree to another and made lovely bridges of themselves. There were neither leaves nor roses on them now, and Mary did not know whether they were dead or alive, but their thin grey or brown branches and sprays looked like a sort of hazy mantle spreading over everything, walls, and trees, and even brown grass, where they had fallen from their fastenings and run along the ground. It was this hazy tangle from tree to tree which made it look so mysterious. Mary had thought it must be different from other gardens which had not been left all by themselves so long; and, indeed, it was different from any other place she had ever seen in her life.

'How still it is!' she whispered. 'How still!'
Then she waited a moment and listened at

Walled garden at Wootton Place
Oxfordshire, England

the stillness. The robin, who had flown to his tree-top, was still as all the rest. He did not even flutter his wings; he sat without stirring, and looked at Mary.

'No wonder it is still,' she whispered again. 'I am the first person who has spoken in here for ten years.'

She moved away from the door, stepping as softly as if she were afraid of awakening some-one. She was glad that there was grass under her feet and that her steps made no sounds. She walked under one of the fairy-like arches between the trees and looked up at the sprays and tendrils which formed them.

'I wonder if they are all quite dead,' she said. 'Is it all a quite dead garden? I wish it wasn't.'

If she had been Ben Weatherstaff she could have told whether the wood was alive by look-ing at it, but she could only see that there were only grey or brown sprays and branches, and none showed any signs of even a tiny leaf-bud anywhere.

But she was *inside* the wonderful garden,

and she could come through the door under the ivy any time, and she felt as if she had found a world all her own.

The sun was shining inside the four walls and the high arch of blue sky over this particular piece of Misselthwaite seemed even more brilliant and soft than it was over the moor. The robin flew down from his tree-top and hopped about or flew after her from one bush to another. He chirped a good deal and had a very busy air, as if he were showing her things. Everything was strange and silent, and she seemed to be hundreds of miles away from anyone, but somehow she did not feel lonely at all. All that troubled her was her wish that she knew whether all the roses were dead, or if perhaps some of them had lived and might put out leaves and buds as the weather got warmer. She did not want it to be a quite dead garden. If it were a quite alive garden, how wonderful it would be, and what thousands of roses would grow on every side?

Her skipping-rope had hung over her arm when she came in, and after she had walked about for a while she thought she would skip round the whole garden, stopping when she wanted to look at things. There seemed to have been grass paths here and there, and in one or two corners there were alcoves of evergreen with stone seats or all moss-covered flower-urns in them.

HUGH
PALMER

Winter aconites (*Eranthis hyemalis*)
at Heale House
Hampshire, England

As she came near the second of these alcoves she stopped skipping. There had once been a flower-bed in it, and she thought she saw something sticking out of the black earth— some sharp little pale green points. She remembered what Ben Weatherstaff had said, and she knelt down to look at them.

'Yes, they are tiny growing things and they *might* be crocuses or snowdrops or daffodils,' she whispered.

She bent very close to them and sniffed the fresh scent of the damp earth. She liked it very much.

'Perhaps there are some other ones coming up in other places,' she said. 'I will go all over the garden and look.'

She did not skip, but walked. She went slowly and kept her eyes on the ground. She looked in the old border-beds and among the grass, and after she had gone round, trying to miss nothing, she had found ever so many more sharp, pale green points, and she had become quite excited again.

'It isn't a quite dead garden,' she cried out softly to herself. 'Even if the roses are dead, there are other things alive.'

She did not know anything about gardening, but the grass seemed so thick in some of the places where the green points were pushing their way through that she thought they did not seem to have room enough to grow. She searched about until she found a rather sharp piece of wood and knelt down and dug and weeded out the weeds and grass until she made nice clear places around them.

'Now they look as if they could breathe,' she said, after she had finished with the first ones. 'I am going to do ever so many more. I'll do all I can see. If I haven't time today I can come tomorrow.'

She went from place to place, and dug and weeded, and enjoyed herself so immensely that she was led on from bed to bed and into the grass under the trees. The exercise made her so warm that she first threw her coat off, and then her hat, and without knowing it she was smiling down on to the grass and the pale green points all the time.

The robin was tremendously busy. He was very much pleased to see gardening begun on his own estate. He had often wondered at Ben Weatherstaff. Where gardening is done all sorts of delightful things to eat are turned up with the soil. Now here was this new kind of creature who was not half Ben's size and yet had the sense to come into his garden and begin at once.

Mistress Mary worked in her garden until it was time to go to her midday dinner. In fact she was rather late in remembering, and when she put on her coat and hat and picked up her skipping-rope, she could not believe that she had been working two or three hours. She had been actually happy all the time; and dozens and dozens of the tiny, pale green points were to be seen in cleared places, looking twice as cheerful as they had looked before when the grass and weeds had been smothering them.

'I shall come back this afternoon,' she said, looking all round at her new kingdom, and speaking to the trees and rose-bushes as if they heard her.

Then she ran lightly across the grass, pushed open the slow old door, and slipped through it under the ivy.

—FROM *THE SECRET GARDEN*

First, gather a great quantity of violet flowers and pick them clean from the stalks and set them on the fire and put to them so much rose water as you think good. Then let them boil all together untill the colour be forth of them, then take them off the fire and strain them through a fine cloth, then put so much sugar to them as you think good, then set it againe to the fire until it be somewhat thick and put it into a violet glasse.

—FROM *THE GOOD HOUSE WIFE'S JEWELL*

KEN DRUSE

Viola 'Freckles' and lungwort
(*Pulmonaria saccharata*)
Near Morristown, New Jersey

Cherry blossoms and azaleas at
Wing Haven Gardens
Charlotte, North Carolina

CHERRY BLOSSOMS

MOTO-ORI NORINAGA

Setting aside my worldly affairs,
    On the cherry-bloom I will gaze,
Every day till it withers; for
    The flowers will last so few days.

SONNET 5

RAINER MARIA RILKE

Flower-muscle, that opens the anemone's
meadow-morning bit by bit,
until into her lap the polyphonic
light of the loud skies pours down,

muscle of infinite reception
tensed in the still star of the blossom,
sometimes *so* overmanned with abundance
that the sunset's beckoning to rest

is scarcely able to give back to you
the wide-sprung petal-edges:
you, resolve and strength of *how many* worlds!

We, with our violence, are longer-lasting.
But *when*, in which one of all lives,
are we at last open and receivers?

—FROM *SONNETS TO ORPHEUS*

I am like the little anemone I once saw in the garden in Rome, which had opened so far during the day that it could no longer close at night! It was dreadful to see it in the dark meadow, wide open, how it still absorbed into its seemingly frantically torn open calyx, with so much too much night above it, and would not be done. And beside it all its clever little sisters, each gone shut through its little measure of abundance. I too am turned so help-lessly outward, hence distraught too by every-thing, refusing nothing, my senses overflowing without asking me to every disturbance; if there is a noise, I give myself up and *am* that noise, and since everything once adjusted to stimula-tion wants to be stimulated, so at bottom I want to be disturbed and am so without end . . . all kindness of people and of Nature remains wasted on me.

—FROM RILKE'S LETTER OF JUNE, 1914

HUGH
PALMER

Windflowers (*Anemone blanda*) at
Sarsden Glebe
Oxfordshire, England

K E N   D R U S E

Trillium grandiflorum 'Flore Pleno' at
Garden in the Woods
Framingham, Massachusetts

FLOWERS AND INSECTS

CHARLES M. SKINNER

Did it ever come into your head that you were going to like something from merely hearing its name? When I was convalescing from an illness in my youth it occurred to me that I wanted a charlotte russe. I had never seen or tasted one of those confections; I hardly knew it from an oyster; but I longed for it—because I did. Invalids have that privilege. My parents went to a baker and had one made. It was one quart in content, and I ate it greedily to the last crumb, and have never cared much for charlotte russe since. Sometimes this gustatory exploit recurs to me when I find myself desiring with an equal ardor of sympathy or curiosity to own some object of natural interest or beauty. There was a crystal of epidote, for instance, that had to be got for my little group of minerals. Why epidote more than rhodonite or dioptase, I do not know, unless it be that the name happened to be remembered from seeing a labeled specimen in childhood.

And so it was with the trillium. I had never seen one, yet I cared a good deal more for it than for a lilium. As I was more than forty years old before I saw one, there should have been a lack of enthusiasm in getting it; but the exuberance of youth came over me at the moment, and I never coddled anything into health with more care than I did that waxen flower and its broad, frank setting, after I had lodged it in a shady corner of my city yard. Was it the name that made me like it? Trillium! There is music in it; there is a sense of wildness; it ripples on the tongue; it has cadence, and somehow it suggests the woods. As in all spring flowers, there is refinement in it, a delicacy and modesty; but unlike most of the blossoms of its season, it has dignity and substance. Its petals are large for the time. If it belongs to the rank of floral infants, it is at least one of those big, healthy, composed infants that are born at an advanced age and are advising their elders at five. What is of moment, it blooms and flourishes in the wild corner of our yard.

—FROM *NATURE IN A CITY YARD*

Of Daffodils there are almost an hundred sorts…every one to be distinguished from other, both in their times, formes, and colours, some being either white, or yellow, or mixt, or else being small or great, single or double, and some having but one flower upon a stalke, or many upon a stalke, that one or two stalkes of flowres are in stead of a whole nose-gay, or bundell of flowers tied together. This I doe affirme upon good knowledge and certaine experience, and not as a great many others doe, tell of the wonders of another world, which themselves never saw nor ever heard of, except from superficiall relation, which themselves have augmented according to their own fansie and conceit.

Againe, let me also by the way tell you, that many idle and ignorant Gardiners and others, who get names by stealth, as they doe many other things, doe call some of these Daffodils Narcisses, when as all know that knowe any Latine, that Narcissus is the Latine name, and Daffodill the English of one and the same thing; and therefore alone without any other Epithete cannot properly distinguish severall things. I would willingly therefore that you all would grow judicious, and call every thing by his proper English name in speaking English, or else by such Latine name as every thing hath that hath not a proper English name, and thereby they may distinguish the severall varieties of things and not confound them, as also to take away all excuses of mistaking, as for example, the single English bastard Daffodill (which groweth wilde in many Woods, Groves, and Orchards in England). The double English bastard Daffodill. The French single white Daffodill, many upon a stalke. The French double yellow Daffodill. The great, or the little, or the least Spanish yellow bastard Daffodill, or the great or little Spanish white Daffodill. The Turkie single white Daffodill, or the Turkie single or double white Daffodill, many upon a stalke.

—PREFACE TO *THE GARDEN OF
PLEASANT FLOWERS*

DAFFODOWNDILLY

A. A. MILNE

She wore her yellow sun-bonnet,
    She wore her greenest gown;
She turned to the south wind
    And curtsied up and down.
She turned to the sunlight
    And shook her yellow head,
And whispered to her neighbor:
    'Winter is dead.'
—FROM *WHEN WE WERE VERY YOUNG*

MICK HALES

Garden of daffodils
Amagansett, New York

Perhaps you'd like to buy a flower,
But I could never sell—
If you would like to *borrow*,
Until the Daffodil

Unties her yellow Bonnet
Beneath the village door,
Until the Bees, from Clover rows
Their Hock, and Sherry, draw,

Why, I will lend until just then,
But not an hour more!

HARRY
HARALAMBOU

Narcissus 'April Tears'
Peconic, New York

APRIL

H E N R Y N . E L L A C O M B E

And though Shakespeare called it 'spongy April,' he also called it 'well-apparelled April,' and 'proud-pied April,' and it is indeed so rich in flowers that it is not easy to select one which demands more attention than others; but in my garden the Fritillaries are a chief ornament in April, and a great delight. I know that they are capricious, and in some gardens they will not grow at all, but here they are quite hardy, and being let alone they increase freely both by their roots and seeds. There are a very large number of species (more than fifty, besides varieties), and I believe they may all be considered hardy, at least in the south of England, and are all well worth growing; but I can only find space for two, which, though the most old-fashioned, are, as I think, the most beautiful. First, there is our own native fritillary; and its popularity is shown by its many English names—such as, death bell, dead man's bell, chequered daffodil, lily, or tulip, drooping tulip, guinea-hen flower, turkey-hen flower, snake's flower, snake's head, and many others. On these I need say nothing; but the Latin name—*Fritillaria meleagris*—deserves a short note. The flower was sent to Clusius, towards the end of the sixteenth century, by Noel Caperon, an apothecary of Orleans, who at the same time suggested that it should be called fritillaria, from *fritillus*, which he supposed to be a chessboard,

instead of the dice-box often used with such a board. Clusius and others, who were better acquainted with Latin, pointed out the mistake, and some suggested *Caperonia*, and others (as Laurembergius) suggested *Gaviana*, from *gavia*, a sea-gull; but *Fritillaria* held its ground, not only as the scientific name, but also as the common name, though Parkinson and others tried to establish the pretty name of chequered daffodil, but in vain. The other name—*Meleagris*—it gets from its likeness to a guinea-hen, and this name it has had for more than three centuries. It is a plant that spreads from Norway through the whole of Central Europe to the Caucasus and Bosnia, and is now admitted into the English flora, but is a doubtful native. It is, however, found sparingly in many parts of England south of the Trent, and may be said to be abundant in the meadows bordering the Thames, from its rise to below Oxford, and in many meadows it is so abundant as fully to justify Matthew Arnold's description:

> I know what white, what purple fritillaries
> The grassy harvest of the river-fields
> Above by Ensham, down by Sandford yields.
> —*Thyrsis*

In some meadows, especially near Cricklade, nearly all the flowers are white, and near

HUGH
PALMER

Checkered lilies (*Fritillaria
Meleagris*) at Old Rectory Cottage
in Tidmarsh
Buckinghamshire, England

Cirencester a curious variety has been found, in which the white flowers and the leaves and flower-stalks are so twisted as to have gained for the plant the name of *F. contorta*. As a garden-flower for April the fritillary is a most desirable plant; however much it spreads and increases it never is in the way: and the leaves and flower-stems die away so soon after the flowering is over that it may be allowed to remain undisturbed in any garden.

—FROM *IN A GLOUCESTERSHIRE GARDEN*

FORGET-ME-NOT

ANONYMOUS

When to the flowers so beautiful
The Father gave a name,
There came a little blue-eyed one
(All timidly it came).
And standing by the Father's side
And gazing in His face
It said in low and trembling tones
Yet with a gentle grace,
"Dear Lord, the name thou gavest me,
Alas! I have forgot"
Kindly the Father looked Him down
And said, "Forget-me-not."

PING
AMRANAND

Forget-me-nots, double-flowered
tulips, and Iceland poppies at
Virginia House
Richmond, Virginia

T U L I P S

S Y L V I A   P L A T H

The tulips are too excitable, it is winter here.
Look how white everything is, how quiet, how snowed-in.
I am learning peacefulness, lying by myself quietly
As the light lies on these white walls, this bed, these hands.
I am nobody; I have nothing to do with explosions.
I have given my name and my day-clothes up to the nurses
And my history to the anesthetist and my body to surgeons.

They have propped my head between the pillow and the sheet-cuff
Like an eye between two white lids that will not shut.
Stupid pupil, it has to take everything in.
The nurses pass and pass, they are no trouble,
They pass the way gulls pass inland in their white caps,
Doing things with their hands, one just the same as another,
So it is impossible to tell how many there are.

My body is a pebble to them, they tend it as water
Tends to the pebbles it must run over, smoothing them gently.
They bring me numbness in their bright needles, they bring me sleep.
Now I have lost myself I am sick of baggage —
My patent leather overnight case like a black pillbox,
My husband and child smiling out of the family photo;
Their smiles catch onto my skin, little smiling hooks.

I have let things slip, a thirty-year-old cargo boat
Stubbornly hanging on to my name and address.
They have swabbed me clear of my loving associations.
Scared and bare on the green plastic-pillowed trolley
I watched my teaset, my bureaus of linen, my books
Sink out of sight, and the water went over my head.
I am a nun now, I have never been so pure.

HUGH
PALMER

Tulips from Covent Garden Market
London, England

I didn't want any flowers, I only wanted
To lie with my hands turned up and be utterly empty.
How free it is, you have no idea how free —
The peacefulness is so big it dazes you,
And it asks nothing, a name tag, a few trinkets.
It is what the dead close on, finally; I imagine them
Shutting their mouths on it, like a Communion tablet.

The tulips are too red in the first place, they hurt me.
Even through the gift paper I could hear them breathe
Lightly, through their white swaddlings, like an awful baby.
Their redness talks to my wound, it corresponds.
They are subtle: they seem to float, though they weigh me down,
Upsetting me with their sudden tongues and their color,
A dozen red lead sinkers round my neck.

Nobody watched me before, now I am watched.
The tulips turn to me, and the window behind me
Where once a day the light slowly widens and slowly thins,
And I see myself, flat, ridiculous, a cut-paper shadow
Between the eye of the sun and the eyes of the tulips,
And I have no face, I have wanted to efface myself.
The vivid tulips eat my oxygen.

Before they came the air was calm enough,
Coming and going, breath by breath, without any fuss.
Then the tulips filled it up like a loud noise.
Now the air snags and eddies round them the way a river
Snags and eddies round a sunken rust-red engine.
They concentrate my attention, that was happy
Playing and resting without committing itself.

The walls, also, seem to be warming themselves.
The tulips should be behind bars like dangerous animals;
They are opening like the mouth of some great African cat,
And I am aware of my heart: it opens and closes
Its bowl of red blooms out of sheer love of me.
The water I taste is warm and salt, like the sea,
And comes from a country far away as health.

PEAS OF THE SEEDY BUDS OF TULIPS

SIR KENELM DIGBY

In the Spring (about the beginning of May) the flowry leaves of Tulips do fall away, and there remains within them the end of the stalk, which in time will turn to seed. Take that seedy end (then very tender) and pick from it the little excresscencies about it, and cut it into short pieces, and boil them and dress them as you would do Pease; and they will taste like Pease, and be very savoury.

HARRY
HARALAMBOU

Tulipa 'Jacqueline' and bleeding
heart (*Dicentra spectabilis*)
Peconic, New York

FLOWERS OF "OUR LADY"

ELIZABETH TODD NASH

It is rather interesting to see how many of the flowers were dedicated to the Virgin Mary or "Our Lady." This is only a partial list, made as they were found in flower lore.

Our Lady's Bedstraw, which filled the manger in which the child Jesus was laid—The Virgin's bed is said to have been made of the Thyme—the Woodruff and Groundsel.

Our Lady's Smock—	Cuckoo flower
Our Lady's Slipper—	Orchid
Our Lady's Garters—	Ribbon grass
Our Lady's Thread—	Dodder
Our Lady's Tresses—	Lady tresses
Our Lady's Tears—	Snowdrop
Our Lady's Milk wort—	Lung wort
Our Lady's Finger—	Amaryllis
Our Lady's Hand—	Orchids from hand shaped roots

Our Lady's Mint (in France)—	Spearmint
Our Lady's Balsam (in Germany)—	Costmary
Our Lady's Keys—	Cowslip
Our Lady's Gloves (in France)—	Digitalis
Our Lady's Night-cap—	Convolvulus and Canterbury bell
Our Lady's Thimble—	Harebell
Our Lady's Hair—	Maiden-hair fern
Our Lady's Flower—	Mary-bud or Marigold

To the Annunciation is appropriated the White Iris, Narcissus, White and blossoming Almond.

To the Visitation—Roses, white and red.

To the Feast of the Assumption—Virgin's bower or Clematis.

—FROM ONE HUNDRED AND ONE
LEGENDS OF FLOWERS

PING
AMRANAND

Clematis at Oatlands
Leesburg, Virginia

47

L I L A C S

A M Y   L O W E L L

Lilacs,
False blue,
White,
Purple,
Color of lilac,
Your great puffs of flowers
Are everywhere in this my New England.
Among your heart-shaped leaves
Orange orioles hop like music-box birds and sing
Their little weak soft songs;
In the crooks of your branches
The bright eyes of song sparrows sitting on spotted eggs
Peer restlessly through the light and shadow
Of all Springs.
Lilacs in dooryards
Holding quiet conversations with an early moon;
Lilacs watching a deserted house
Settling sideways into the grass of an old road;
Lilacs, wind-beaten, staggering under a lopsided shock of bloom
Above a cellar dug into a hill.
You are everywhere.
You were everywhere.
You tapped the window when the preacher preached his sermon,
And ran along the road beside the boy going to school.
You stood by pasture-bars to give the cows good milking,
You persuaded the housewife that her dish-pan was of silver
And her husband an image of pure gold.
You flaunted the fragrance of your blossoms
Through the wide doors of Custom Houses—
You, and sandalwood, and tea,
Charging the noses of quill-driving clerks
When a ship was in from China.
You called to them: "Goose-quill men, goose-quill men,
May is a month for flitting,"

Until they writhed on their high stools
And wrote poetry on their letter-sheets behind the propped-up ledgers.
Paradoxical New England clerks,
Writing inventories in ledgers, reading the "Song of Solomon" at night,
So many verses before bedtime,
Because it was the Bible.
The dead fed you
Amid the slant stones of graveyards.
Pale ghosts who planted you
Came in the night time
And let their thin hair blow through their clustered stems.
You are of the green sea,
And of the stone hills which reach a long distance.
You are of elm-shaded streets with little shops where they sell kites and marbles,
You are of great parks where everyone walks and nobody is at home.
You cover the blind sides of greenhouses
And lean over the top to say a hurry-word through the glass
To your friends, the grapes, inside.

Lilacs,
False blue,
White,
Purple,
Color of lilac,
You have forgotten your Eastern origin,
The veiled women with eyes like panthers,
The swollen, aggressive turbans of jeweled Pashas.
Now you are a very decent flower,
A reticent flower,
A curiously clear-cut, candid flower,
Standing beside clean doorways,
Friendly to a house-cat and a pair of spectacles,
Making poetry out of a bit of moonlight
And a hundred or two sharp blossoms.

Maine knows you,
Has for years and years;
New Hampshire knows you,
And Massachusetts

MICK HALES

Lilacs at Glynwood Farms
Cold Spring, New York

And Vermont.

Cape Cod starts you along the beaches to Rhode Island;

Connecticut takes you from a river to the sea.

You are brighter than apples,

Sweeter than tulips,

You are the great flood of our souls

Bursting above the leaf-shapes of our hearts,

You are the smell of all Summers,

The love of wives and children,

The recollection of the gardens of little children,

You are State Houses and Charters

And the familiar treading of the foot to and fro on a road it knows.

May is lilac here in New England,

May is a thrush singing "Sun up!" on a tip-top ash-tree,

May is white clouds behind pine-trees

Puffed out and marching upon a blue sky.

May is a green as no other,

May is much sun through small leaves,

May is soft earth,

And apple-blossoms,

And windows open to a South wind.

May is a full light wind of lilac

From Canada to Narragansett Bay.

Lilacs,

False blue,

White,

Purple,

Color of lilac,

Heart-leaves of lilac all over New England,

Roots of lilac under all the soil of New England,

Lilac in me because I am New England,

Because my roots are in it,

Because my leaves are of it,

Because my flowers are for it,

Because it is my country

And I speak to it of itself

And sing of it with my own voice

Since certainly it is mine.

CHEDDAR PINKS

ROBERT BRIDGES

Mid the squander'd colour
    idling as I lay
Reading the Odyssey
    in my rock-garden
I espied the cluster'd
    tufts of Cheddar pinks
Burgeoning with promise
    of their scented bloom
All the modish motley
    of their bloom to-be
Thrust up in narrow buds
    on the slender stalks
Thronging springing urgent
    hasting (so I thought)
As if they feared to be
    too late for summer—
Like schoolgirls overslept
    waken'd by the bell
Leaping from bed to don
    their muslin dresses
        On a May morning:

Then felt I like to one
    indulging in sin
(Whereto Nature is oft
    a blind accomplice)
Because my aged bones
    so enjoyed the sun
There as I lay along
    idling with my thoughts
Reading an old poet
    while the busy world

PETER
MARGONELLI

Maiden pinks (*Dianthus deltoides*)
Northwestern Connecticut

Toil'd moil'd fuss'd and scurried
   worried bought and sold
Plotted stole and quarrel'd
   fought and God knows what
I had forgotten Homer
   dallying with my thoughts
Till I fell to making
   these little verses
Communing with the flowers
   in my rock-garden
      On a May morning.

PING
AMRANAND

Dogwoods and azaleas at the
National Arboretum
Washington, D.C.

THE FRANKLIN'S TALE

So on a day, right in the morwe tyde,
Unto a gardyne that was ther besyde,
In which that thay hadde made here ordinaunce
Of vitaile, and of other purvyaunce,
They gon and pleyen hem al the longe day.
And this was on the sixte morwe of May,
Which May had peynted with his softe schoures
This gardyn ful of leves and of floures.

So on a day, before the sun was high,
Unto a garden fair that was hard by
(Wherein they had spread forth their meat and drink,
And every comfort that the heart could think),
They went—and sported all the whole long day,
And this was on the sixth sweet morn of May,
When May had painted, with his tender showers,
This garden full of fragrant leaves and flowers.

—FROM *THE CANTERBURY TALES*

PING
AMRANAND

Lavender split-petal azaleas
(*Rhododendron* 'Koromo Shikubu')
and statue of Pan at Hillwood
Washington, D.C.

55

DANDELIONS

LOUIS MACNEICE

Incorrigible, brash,
They brightened the cinder path of my childhood,
Unsubtle, the opposite of primroses,
But, unlike primroses, capable
Of growing anywhere, railway track, pierhead,
Like our extrovert friends who never
Make us fall in love, yet fill
The primroseless roseless gaps.

—FROM "NATURE NOTES"

PING
AMRANAND

Dandelion and magnolia petals at
the National Arboretum
Washington, D.C.

THE WAYS OF WISTARIA

COLETTE

I hope that it is still alive, and that it will go on living for a long time, that flourishing, irrepressible despot, a centenarian at least twice over: the wistaria that spills over the garden walls of the house where I was born, and down into the rue des Vignes. Proof of its vitality was brought to me last year by a spry and charming lady pillager . . . A black dress, a head of white hair, a sexagenarian agility—all this had jumped, in the rue des Vignes, deserted as in bygone days, until it had grabbed hold of and made off with one of the wistaria's long terminal withes, which ended up flowering in Paris, on the divan bed where I am bound by my arthritis. Besides its fragrance, the butterfly-shaped flower retained a small hymenoptera, an inchworm, and a ladybug, all direct and unexpected from Saint-Sauveur, in Puisaye.

To tell the truth about this wistaria, in which I discovered, here on by bed table, a fragrance, a blue-violet color, and a bearing all vaguely recognizable, I remember that it had a bad reputation all along that narrow domain bounded by a wall and defended by an iron railing. It dates from long ago, from before my mother Sido's first marriage. Its mad profusion in May and its meager resurgence in August and September perfume my earliest childhood memories. It was as heavy with bees as with blossoms and would hum like a cymbal whose sound spreads without ever fading away, more

beautiful each year, until the time when Sido, leaning over its flowery burden out of curiosity, let out the little "Ah-hah!" of great discoveries long anticipated: the wistaria had begun to pull up the iron railing.

As there could be no question, in Sido's domain, of killing a wistaria, it exercised, and exercises still, its decided strength. I saw it lift an impressive length of railing up out of the stone and mortar, brandish it in the air, bend the bars in plantlike imitation of its own twists and turns, and show a marked preference for an ophidian intertwining of bar and trunk, eventually embedding the one in the other. In time it met up with its neighbor the honeysuckle, the sweet, charming, red-flowered honeysuckle. At first it seemed not to notice, and then slowly smothered it as a snake suffocates a bird.

As I watched, I learned that its overwhelming beauty served a murderous strength. I learned how it covers, strangles, adorns, ruins, and shores up. The Ampelopsis is a mere boy compared with the coils, woody even when new, of the wistaria . . .

I visited the Désert de Retz one beautiful, torrid day when everything conspired toward a siesta and disturbing dreams. I will never go back there, for fear of finding that that place, made for tempered nightmares, has paled. Muddy, rush-filled water slept there at the foot of a kiosk furnished with broken-down writing

HUGH
PALMER

Wisteria sinensis at Wardington Manor
Oxfordshire, England

59

tables, footless stools, and other unexplained pieces of furniture floating around. I cling to the memory of a truncated tower, topped off abruptly by a beveled roof. Inside, it was divided into little cells around a spiral staircase, each of which assumed, roughly, the shape of a trapezoid . . .

O world, how full you are of mysteries and inconveniences for one by no means a born geometrician, struggling in vain to describe the truncated tower of the Désert de Retz. It was crammed with ruined furniture. Should I laugh at their skeletons or fear that one of life's baleful remnants . . .

The sudden shattering of a windowpane made me shudder, and decided it: a vegetable arm, crooked, twisted, in which I had no difficulty recognizing the workings, the surreptitious approach, the reptilian mind of the wistaria, had just struck, broken, and entered.

—FROM *FLOWERS AND FRUIT*

HUGH PALMER

Wisteria sinensis at the Generalife
Granada, Spain

61

RICARDO REIS
(FERNANDO PESSOA)

I prefer roses to my country,
And I love magnolias more,
Beloved, than glory or virtue.

So long as life does not weary me,
I give it leave to pass me by,
So long as I remain the same.

He who no longer knows care, what cares he
That one should win, another lose,
If dawn breaks nonetheless,

If every year when spring returns
The leaves unfold
And die with autumn-tide?

What of the rest, those other things
With which men supplement this life,
What do they add to my soul?

Nothing, save a wish for unconcern,
And soft surrender
To the fleeting hour.

PING
AMRANAND

Magnolia Yulan at Dumbarton Oaks
Washington, D.C.

THE MAGNOLIA

FRANCIS PONGE

The magnolia blossom erupts in slow motion like a leisurely
bubble on the thick skin of syrup that's turning to caramel.
(The caramel color of the leaves on the tree should be noted too.)
Once in full bloom, it represents total satisfaction, in keeping
with the significant vegetal mass expressed there.
But it is not sticky; quite the contrary, it is cool and silky, in
the same measure that the leaf seems glistening, coppery, dry and
brittle.

HUGH
PALMER

Iris pallida and *Euphorbia Wulfenii*
at Tintinhull
Somerset, England

64

LET'S MAKE A FLOWER GARDEN

HANNA RION

The iris called "German" is, strange to say, the model of the French design of fleur-de-lis. Though of very old lineage, many modern frills have been added to the original white and purple "flags" of our grandfathers. I love them even more than the aristocratic hypenated Japanese ones, because they are not proud but will flourish all over the garden, and they haven't any "varmints"; and above all, they have the most decorative form in all the flower world.

I have often wondered why these irises are called "flags." In wondering aloud to a Frenchman the other day I accidentally found why. It seems that in Normandy the *chaumière* or thatched cottage is given a finish, a foot wide, of clay, extending the entire length of roof peak. This is primarily for the purpose of preventing leaks, but it serves, generally, the more charming purpose of making a roof garden, for along the entire length of this ridgepole of clay sod, over the thatch, are planted these irises. From the pinnacle of roof the flowers float in the breeze *like flags.*

—FROM *LET'S MAKE A FLOWER GARDEN*

Long-spurred columbines
(*Aquilegia × hybrida*)
Bronx, New York

THE LANGUAGE OF FLOWERS

Columbine, colored,
Aquelegia.
I CANNOT RESIGN THEE.

Columbine, white,
Aquelegia.
RESOLVED TO WIN.

THE LITTLE GARDEN
AND THE PEONY

MRS. EDWARD HARDING

No garden can really be too small to hold a peony. Had I but four square feet of ground at my disposal, I would plant a peony in the centre and proceed to worship....

In March of 1919 I had a wonderful opportunity to see the battle-fronts of Europe from Nancy to Ostend. A sadder, more appalling vision of destruction never was. Town after town was leveled to heaps of brick and dust;

PING
AMRANAND

Paeonia 'Festiva Maxima' and sundial
Washington, D.C.

tree after tree was deliberately sawed off and left to rot. The grapevines were pulled up, the fruit trees girdled, the land itself so shattered and upheaved that the gardener's first query was whether it could again bear crops before the lapse of many years.

We had left Amiens one Sunday morning, and passing Villers-Bretoneaux—where the Australian troops and some American engineers had made the stand that saved Amiens and the Western line—had gone through Hamelet, Hamel, Bayonvillers, Harbonnières, and Crepy Wood to Vauvillers. As the only woman in the party, I had been unanimously appointed in charge of the commissariat. It was noon when we reached Vauvillers. I chose a broken wall about fifty feet from the road as a good place on which to spread our luncheon. The car was stopped, the luncheon things were unpacked, and we picked our way over the mangled ground to the fragment of wall. As I passed around the end I came upon two peony plants pushing through the earth. Tears brimmed. I could not control them. Here had been a home and a cherished garden. As I stood gazing at the little red spears just breaking through the ground, a voice, apparently from the sky,

inquired whether Madame would like a chair. Looking along the wall I saw the head of an old peasant woman thrust through a tiny opening. She smiled and withdrew, appearing a moment later with a chair. It was her only chair. She then brought forth her only cup and saucer, her only pitcher filled with milk, and offered us her only hospitality!

Joined now by her venerable husband, we listened to their story. The hiding of their few treasures, the burial of their bit of linen, their flight toward Paris, the description of the outrageous condition of the one room left for them to return to, made us burn with indignation. It was in her little garden that the peonies grew. The fruit trees and shrubs were gone, the neat garden walks were blasted into space, the many precious flowers were utterly destroyed. When she found that Madame, too, loved *les belles pivoines*, she urged me to take one of the only two roots she had left!

We went away leaving the old couple laden with supplies, and I gathered from every man in our party a heavy toll of tobacco for a farewell gift of comfort. I hope she has again a little garden, with all the peonies it will hold.

—FROM *PEONIES IN THE LITTLE GARDEN*

MICK HALES

The West Garden at Hatfield House
Hertfordshire, England

WHAT AILS MY FERN?

JAMES SCHUYLER

My peonies have lovely leaves
but rarely flower.
Oh, they have buds
and plenty of them. These
grow to the size of peas
and stay
that way.
Is this
bud blast?

What ails my fern?

I enclose a sample
of a white disease
on a leaf
of honesty
known also
as the money plant

My two blue spruce
look worse and worse

What ails my fern?

Two years ago a tenant
wound tape around my tree.
Sap dripped out of the branches
on babies in buggies below. So
I unwound the tape.
Can nothing be done
to revive my tree?

PETER C
JONES

Mock orange (*Philadelphus
coronarius*) and perennial geraniums
Coastal Rhode Island

70

What ails my fern?

I hate my disordered
backyard fence
where lilac, weigela
and mock orange grow.
Please advise
how to get rid of it.

Weeping willow roots
reaching out
seeking water
fill my cesspool and well.
What do you suggest?

What ails my fern?

SUMMER

AN ISLAND GARDEN

CELIA THAXTER

I muse over their seed-pods, those supremely graceful urns that are wrought with such matchless elegance of shape, and think what strange power they hold within. Sleep is there, and Death his brother, imprisoned in those mystic sealed cups. There is a hint of their mystery in their shape of sombre beauty, but never a suggestion in the fluttering blossom; it is the gayest flower that blows. In the more delicate varieties the stalks are so slender, yet so strong, like fine grass stems, when you examine them you wonder how they hold even the light weight of the flower so firmly and proudly erect. They are clothed with the finest of fine hairs up and down the stalks, and over the green calyx, especially in the Iceland varieties, where these hairs are of a lovely red-brown color and add much to their beauty.

It is plain to see, as one gazes over the Poppy beds on some sweet evening at sunset, what buds will bloom in the joy of next morning's first sunbeams, for these will be lifting themselves heavenward, slowly and silently, but surely. To stand by the beds at sunrise and see the flowers awake is a heavenly delight. As the first long, low rays of the sun strike the buds, you know they feel the signal! A light air stirs among them; you lift your eyes, perhaps to look at a rosy cloud or follow the flight of a caroling bird, and when you look back again, lo! the calyx has fallen from the largest bud and lies on the ground, two half transparent, light green shells, leaving the flower petals wrinkled in a thousand folds, just released from their close pressure. A moment more and they are unclosing before your eyes. They flutter out on the gentle breeze like silken banners to the sun, and such a color! The orange of the Iceland Poppy is the most ineffable color; it "warms the wind" indeed! I know no tint like it; it is orange dashed with carmine, most like the reddest coals of an intensely burning fire. Look at this exquisite cup: the wind has blown nearly smooth the crinkled petals; these, where they meet in the center, melt into a delicate greenish yellow. In the heart of the blossom rises a round green altar, its sides penciled with nine black lines, and a nine-rayed star of yellow velvet clasps the flat, pure green top. From the base of this altar springs the wreath of stamens and anthers; the inner circle of these is generally white, the outer yellow, and all held high and clear within the cup. The radiant effect of this arrangement against the living red cannot be told.

—FROM *AN ISLAND GARDEN*

KEN DRUSE

Poppy seed capsules
Washington, Connecticut

PING
AMRANAND

Iceland poppies at Virginia House
Richmond, Virginia

CONTENT IN A GARDEN

CANDACE WHEELER

Many gardens may have been planted to secure an effect of gradation in color, but my first thought of it came to me years ago in a place I like to remember. A great part of the beauty of Mrs. Thaxter's house in the Isles of Shoals was made up of flowers. It was far more enjoyable than her garden, where the flowers grew luxuriantly at their own sweet wills, or at the will of the planter, never troubling their heads about agreeing with their neighbors. I remember it as a disappointment that a woman with so exquisite a sense of combination and gradation in the arrangement of flowers, should have so little thought of color effect in her garden.

But in the house! I have never anywhere seen such realized possibilities of color! The fine harmonic sense of the woman and artist and poet thrilled through these long chords of color, and filled the room with an atmosphere which made it seem like living in a rainbow.

The tops of the low bookcases, that filled all the wall space not opened in windows to the sea, were massed with her beloved flowers. I remember she told me that at four in the morning, when the sea and sky seemed to be spread for her alone, she was always out gathering them. I like to think of her there—the tall, white figure standing under the sky and beside the sea which laps her much-loved Isles of Shoals, among the flowers in the early morning, which, although bare of humanity, she found full to the brim of the beauty which her soul loved.

—FROM *CONTENT IN A GARDEN*

MICK HALES

Celia Thaxter's garden
Appledore Island, Maine

77

HUGH
PALMER

Lupines at Great Dixter
Sussex, England

PAINTING THE LANDSCAPE

ROSE FAY THOMAS

The exchange of seeds and plants which always attends such garden visits is one of the pleasant incidents connected with them. My garden is a veritable album, and as I wander over our place I find many a dear friend or happy hour commemorated in it. This little clump of oxalis, naturalized so prettily in the woods, was gathered one lovely day when a merry party joined us in an expedition to the Profile Notch. That group of lady's-slippers came from the woods of a dear friend in Vermont. Here are moss roses from a magnificent rose garden in Massachusetts, and there are seedlings from the home of Longfellow, or willows rooted from cuttings brought from the South by Frederick Law Olmsted. Hardly a flower-loving friend have I who has not left an autograph in plant, or shrub, or tree in my garden, and in like manner many a thrifty plant has left my borders for those of distant friends.

—FROM *OUR MOUNTAIN GARDEN*

RICHARD
FELBER

Field of wild lupines
Litchfield, Connecticut

THE TUFT OF FLOWERS

ROBERT FROST

I went to turn the grass once after one
Who mowed it in the dew before the sun.

The dew was gone that made his blade so keen
Before I came to view the leveled scene.

I looked for him behind an isle of trees;
I listened for his whetstone on the breeze.

But he had gone his way, the grass all mown,
And I must be, as he had been,—alone,

'As all must be,' I said within my heart,
'Whether they work together or apart.'

But as I said it swift there passed me by
On noiseless wing a bewildered butterfly,

Seeking with memories grown dim o'er night
Some resting flower of yesterday's delight.

And once I marked his flight go round and round,
As where some flower lay withering on the ground.

And then he flew as far as eye could see,
And then on tremulous wing came back to me.

I thought of questions that have no reply,
And would have turned to toss the grass to dry;

But he turned first, and led my eye to look
At a tall tuft of flowers beside a brook,

A leaping tongue of bloom the scythe had spared
Beside a reedy brook the scythe had bared.

The mower in the dew had loved them thus,
By leaving them to flourish, not for us,

Nor yet to draw one thought of ours to him,
But from sheer morning gladness at the brim.

The butterfly and I had lit upon,
Nevertheless, a message from the dawn,

That made me hear the wakening birds around,
And hear his long scythe whispering to the ground,

And feel a spirit kindred to my own;
So that henceforth I worked no more alone;

But glad with him, I worked as with his aid,
And weary, sought at noon with him the shade;

And dreaming, as it were, held brotherly speech
With one whose thought I had not hoped to reach.

'Men work together,' I told him from the heart,
'Whether they work together or apart.'

CURTICE
TAYLOR

Poppies and wheat
Northern Italy

HUGH
PALMER

Kew Gardens
London, England

KEW GARDENS

VIRGINIA WOOLF

From the oval-shaped flower-bed there rose perhaps a hundred stalks spreading into heart-shaped or tongue-shaped leaves half-way up and unfurling at the tip red or blue or yellow petals marked with spots of colour raised upon the surface; and from the red, blue or yellow gloom of the throat emerged a straight bar, rough with gold dust and slighted clubbed at the end. The petals were voluminous enough to be stirred by the summer breeze, and when they moved, the red, blue and yellow lights passed one over the other, staining an inch of the brown earth beneath with a spot of the most intricate colour. The light fell either upon the smooth, grey back of a pebble, or, the shell of a snail with its brown, circular veins, or falling into a raindrop, it expanded with such intensity of red, blue and yellow the thin walls of water that one expected them to burst and disappear. Instead, the drop was left in a second silver grey once more, and the light now settled upon the flesh of a leaf, revealing the branching thread of fibre beneath the surface, and again it moved on and spread its illumination in the vast green spaces beneath the dome of the heart-shaped and tongue-shaped leaves. Then the breeze stirred rather more briskly overhead and the colour was flashed into the air above, into the eyes of the men and women who walk in Kew Gardens in July.

The figures of these men and women straggled past the flower-bed with a curiously irregular movement not unlike that of the white and blue butterflies who crossed the turf in zig-zag flights from bed to bed. The man was about six inches in front of the woman, strolling carelessly, while she bore on with greater purpose, only turning her head now and then to see that the children were not too far behind. The man kept this distance in front of the woman purposely, though perhaps unconsciously, for he wished to go on with his thoughts.

"Fifteen years ago I came here with Lily," he thought. "We sat somewhere over there by a lake and I begged her to marry me all through the hot afternoon. How the dragonfly kept circling round us: how clearly I see the dragonfly and her shoe with the square silver buckle at the toe. All the time I spoke I saw her shoe and when it moved impatiently I knew without looking up what she was going to say: the whole of her seemed to be in her shoe. And my love, my desire, were in the dragonfly; for some reason I thought that if it settled there, on that leaf, the broad one with the red flower in the middle of it, if the dragonfly settled on the leaf she would say 'Yes' at once. But the dragonfly went round and round: it never settled anywhere—of course not, happily not, or I shouldn't be walking here with Eleanor and the children. Tell me, Eleanor. D'you ever think of the past?"

"Why do you ask, Simon?"

"Because I've been thinking of the past. I've been thinking of Lily, the woman I might have married. . . . Well, why are you silent? Do you mind my thinking of the past?"

"Why should I mind, Simon? Doesn't one always think of the past, in a garden with men and women lying under the trees? Aren't they one's past, all that remains of it, those men and women, those ghosts lying under the trees, . . . one's happiness, one's reality?"

"For me, a square silver shoe buckle and a dragonfly—"

"For me, a kiss. Imagine six little girls sitting before their easels twenty years ago, down by the side of a lake, painting the water-lilies, the first red water-lilies I'd ever seen. And suddenly a kiss, there on the back of my neck. And my hand shook all the afternoon so that I couldn't paint. I took out my watch and marked the hour when I would allow myself to think of the kiss for five minutes only—it was so precious—the kiss of an old grey-haired woman with a wart on her nose, the mother of all my kisses all my life. Come, Caroline, come, Hubert."

They walked on past the flower-bed, now walking four abreast, and soon diminished in size among the trees and looked half transparent as the sunlight and shade swam over their backs in large trembling irregular patches.

In the oval flower-bed the snail, whose shell had been stained red, blue and yellow for the space of two minutes or so, now appeared to be moving very slightly in its shell, and next began to labour over the crumbs of loose earth which broke away and rolled down as it passed over them. It appeared to have a definite goal in front of it, differing in this respect from the singular high stepping angular green insect who attempted to cross in front of it, and waited for a second with its antennae trembling as if in deliberation, and then stepped off as rapidly and strangely in the opposite direction. Brown cliffs with deep green lakes in the hollows, flat, blade-like trees that waved from root to tip, round boulders of grey stone, vast crumpled surfaces of a thin crackling texture—all these objects lay across the snail's progress between one stalk and another to his goal. Before he had decided whether to circumvent the arched tent of a dead leaf or to breast it there came past the bed the feet of other human beings.

This time they were both men. The younger of the two wore an expression of perhaps unnatural calm; he raised his eyes and fixed them very steadily in front of him while his companion spoke, and directly his companion had done speaking he looked on the ground again and sometimes opened his lips only after a long pause and sometimes did not open them at all. The elder man had a curiously uneven and shaky method of walking, jerking his hand forward and throwing up his head abruptly, rather in the manner of an impatient carriage horse tired of waiting outside a house; but in the man these gestures were irresolute and pointless. He talked almost incessantly; he smiled to himself and again began to talk, as if the smile had been an answer. He was talking about spirits—the spirits of the dead, who, according to him, were even now telling him all sorts of odd things about their experiences in Heaven.

"Heaven was known to the ancients as Thessaly, William, and now, with this war, the spirit matter is rolling between the hills like thunder." He paused, seemed to listen, smiled, jerked his head and continued:

"You have a small electric battery and a

piece of rubber to insulate the wire—isolate?—insulate?—well, we'll skip the details, no good going into details that wouldn't be understood—and in short the little machine stands in any convenient position by the head of the bed, we will say, on a neat mahogany stand. All arrangements being properly fixed by workmen under my direction, the widow applies her ear and summons the spirit by sign as agreed. Women! Widows! Women in black—"

Here he seemed to have caught sight of a woman's dress in the distance, which in the shade looked a purple black. He took off his hat, placed his hand upon his heart, and hurried towards her muttering and gesticulating feverishly. But William caught him by the sleeve and touched a flower with the tip of his walking stick in order to divert the old man's attention. After looking at it for a moment in some confusion the old man bent his ear to it and seemed to answer a voice speaking from it, for he began talking about the forests of Uruguay which he had visited hundreds of years ago in company with the most beautiful young woman in Europe. He could be heard murmuring about forests of Uruguay blanketed with the wax petals of tropical roses, nightingales, sea beaches, mermaids, and women drowned at sea, as he suffered himself to be moved on by William, upon whose face the look of stoical patience grew slowly deeper and deeper.

Following his steps so closely as to be slightly puzzled by his gestures came two elderly women of the lower middle class, one stout and ponderous, the other rose cheeked and nimble. Like most people of their station they were frankly fascinated by any signs of eccentricity betokening a disordered brain, especially in the well-to-do; but they were too far off to be certain whether the gestures were merely eccentric or genuinely mad. After they had scrutinized the old man's back in silence for a moment and given each other a queer, sly look, they went on energetically piecing together their very complicated dialogue:

"Nell, Bert, Lot, Cess, Phil, Pa, he says, I says, she says, I says, I says—"

"My Bert, Sis, Bill, Grandad, the old man, sugar,

Sugar, flour, kippers, greens,
Sugar, sugar, sugar."

The ponderous woman looked through the pattern of falling words at the flowers standing cool, firm, and upright in the earth, with a curious expression. She saw them as a sleeper waking from a heavy sleep sees a brass candlestick reflecting the light in an unfamiliar way, and closes his eyes and opens them, and seeing the brass candlestick again, finally starts broad awake and stares at the candlestick with all his powers. So the heavy woman came to a standstill opposite the oval-shaped flower-bed, and ceased even to pretend to listen to what the other woman was saying. She stood there letting the words fall over her, swaying the top part of her body slowly backwards and forwards, looking at the flowers. Then she suggested that they should find a seat and have their tea.

The snail had now considered every possible method of reaching his goal without going round the dead leaf or climbing over it. Let alone the effort needed for climbing a leaf, he was doubtful whether the thin texture which vibrated with such an alarming crackle when touched even by the tips of his horns would bear his weight; and this determined him finally to creep beneath it, for there was a point where the leaf curved high enough from the ground to admit him. He had just inserted his head in the opening and was taking stock of the high brown roof and was getting used to the cool brown light when two other people came past outside on the turf. This time they were both young, a young man and a young woman. They were both in the prime of youth, or even in that season which precedes the prime of youth, the season before the smooth pink folds of the flower have burst their gummy case, when the wings of the butterfly, though fully grown, are motionless in the sun.

"Lucky it isn't Friday," he observed.

"Why? D'you believe in luck?"

"They make you pay sixpence on Friday."

"What's sixpence anyway? Isn't it worth six-pence?"

"What's 'it'—what do you mean by 'it'?"

"O, anything—I mean—you know what I mean."

Long pauses came between each of these remarks; they were uttered in toneless and monotonous voices. The couple stood still on the edge of the flower-bed, and together pressed the end of her parasol deep down into the soft earth. The action and the fact that his hand rested on the top of hers expressed their feelings in a strange way, as these short insignificant words also expressed something, words with short wings for their heavy body of meaning, inadequate to carry them far and thus alighting awkwardly upon the very common objects that surrounded them, and were to their inexperienced touch so massive; but who knows (so they thought as they pressed the parasol into the earth) what precipices aren't concealed in them,

or what slopes of ice don't shine in the sun on the other side? Who knows? Who has ever seen this before? Even when she wondered what sort of tea they gave you at Kew, he felt that something loomed up behind her words, and stood vast and solid behind them; and the mist very slowly rose and uncovered—O, Heavens, what were those shapes?—little white tables, and waitresses who looked first at her and then at him; and there was a bill that he would pay with a real two shilling piece, and it was real, all real, he assured himself, fingering the coin in his pocket, real to everyone except to him and to her; even to him it began to seem real; and then—but it was too exciting to stand and think any longer, and he pulled the parasol out of the earth with a jerk and was impatient to find the place where one had tea with other people, like other people.

"Come along, Trissie; it's time we had our tea."

"Wherever *does* one have one's tea?" she asked with the oddest thrill of excitement in her voice, looking vaguely round and letting herself be drawn on down the grass path, trailing her parasol; turning her head this way and that way forgetting her tea, wishing to go down there and then down there, remembering orchids and cranes among wild flowers, a Chinese pagoda and a crimson crested bird; but he bore her on.

Thus one couple after another with much the same irregular and aimless movement passed the flower-bed and were enveloped in layer after layer of green blue vapour, in which at first their bodies had substance and a dash of colour, but later both substance and colour dissolved in the green-blue atmosphere. How hot it was! So hot that even the thrush chose to hop, like a mechanical bird, in the shadow of the flowers, with long pauses between one movement and the next; instead of rambling vaguely the white butterflies danced one above another, making with their white shifting flakes the outline of a shattered marble column above the tallest flowers; the glass roofs of the palm house shone as if a whole market full of shiny green umbrellas had opened in the sun; and in the drone of the aeroplane the voice of the summer sky murmured its fierce soul. Yellow and black, pink and snow white, shapes of all these colours, men, women, and children were spotted for a second upon the horizon, and then, seeing the breadth of yellow that lay upon the grass, they wavered and sought shade beneath the trees, dissolving like drops of water in the yellow and green atmosphere, staining it faintly with red and blue. It seemed as if all gross and heavy bodies had sunk down in the heat motionless and lay huddled upon the ground, but their voices went wavering from them as if they were flames lolling from the thick waxen bodies of candles. Voices. Yes, voices. Wordless voices, breaking the silence suddenly with such depth of contentment, such passion of desire, or, in the voices of children, such freshness of surprise; breaking the silence? But there was no silence; all the time the motor omnibuses were turning their wheels and changing their gear; like a vast nest of Chinese boxes all of wrought steel turning ceaselessly one within another the city murmured; on the top of which the voices cried aloud and the petals of myriads of flowers flashed their colours into the air.

She opens in the morning
red as blood.
The dew dare not touch her
for it would burn.
At noon, full-blown,
she is hard as coral.
Even the sun at the window
looks in to see her glow.
When the birds begin
to sing among the branches,
and the afternoon faints
on the violets of the sea,
she turns pale, with the pallor
of a cheek of salt.
And when night is blown
on a soft metallic horn,
while the stars advance,
while the winds retreat,
on the very edge of darkness
her petals begin to rain.

—FROM *DOÑA ROSITA,
THE SPINSTER* OR
*THE LANGUAGE
OF THE FLOWERS*

KEN DRUSE

Old-fashioned rose
Northern New Jersey

GERTRUDE STEIN

A pale rose is a smell that has no fountain, that has upside down the same distinction, elegance is not coloured, the pain is there.

—FROM *GEOGRAPHY AND PLAYS*

SONG OF THE ROSE

~~~~~~

W. H. AUDEN

The red garden rose we planted
Has fair and stately grown;
Our fondest hopes were granted.
Scarlet heavy-scented flowers
Beguiled our summer hours:
Blessed those are who a garden own
Where such a rose-tree flowers.

Though, through the pine woods wailing,
The winter wind makes moan,
Its rage is unavailing.
Long before the autumn ended,
Our roof with tiles we mended:
Blessed those are who a roof still own
When such a wind comes wailing.

THE ROSE

IVAN TURGENEV

The last days of August. . . . Autumn was already at hand.

The sun was setting. A sudden downpour of rain, without thunder or lightning, had just passed rapidly over our wide plain.

The garden in front of the house glowed and steamed, all filled with the fire of the sunset and the deluge of rain.

She was sitting at a table in the drawing-room, and, with persistent dreaminess, gazing through the half-open door into the garden.

I knew what was passing that moment in her soul; I knew that, after a brief but agonising struggle, she was at that instant giving herself up to a feeling she could no longer master.

All at once she got up, went quickly out into the garden, and disappeared.

An hour passed . . . a second; she had not returned.

Then I got up, and, getting out of the house, I turned along the walk by which—of that I had no doubt—she had gone.

All was darkness about me; the night had already fallen. But on the damp sand of the path a roundish object could be discerned—bright red even through the mist.

I stooped down. It was a fresh, new-blown rose. Two hours before I had seen this very rose on her bosom.

I carefully picked up the flower that had fallen in the mud, and, going back to the drawing-room, laid it on the table before her chair.

And now at last she came back, and with light footsteps, crossing the whole room, sat down at the table.

Her face was both paler and more vivid; her downcast eyes, that looked somehow smaller, strayed rapidly in happy confusion from side to side.

She saw the rose, snatched it up, glanced at its crushed, muddy petals, glanced at me, and her eyes, brought suddenly to a standstill, were bright with tears.

"What are you crying for?" I asked.

"Why, see this rose. Look what has happened to it."

Then I thought fit to utter a profound remark.

"Your tears will wash away the mud," I pronounced with a significant expression.

"Tears do not wash, they burn," she answered. And turning to the hearth she flung the rose into the dying flame.

"Fire burns even better than tears," she cried with spirit; and her lovely eyes, still bright with tears, laughed boldly and happily.

I saw that she too had been in the fire.

April, 1878

PING
AMRANAND

Rose garden at Dumbarton Oaks
Washington, D.C.

THE GARDEN

ANDREW MARVELL

How vainly men themselves amaze
To win the Palm, the Oke, or Bayes;
And their uncessant Labours see
Crown'd from some single Herb or Tree.
Whose short and narrow verged Shade
Does prudently their Toyles upbraid;
While all Flow'rs and all Trees do close
To weave the Garlands of repose.

Fair quiet, have I found thee here,
And Innocence thy Sister dear?
Mistaken long, I sought you then
In busy Companies of Men.
Your sacred Plants, if here below,
Only among the Plants will grow.
Society is all but rude,
To this delicious Solitude.

No white nor red was ever seen
So am'rous as this lovely green.
Fond Lovers, cruel as their Flame,
Cut in these Trees their Mistress name.
Little, Alas, they know, or heed,
How far these Beauties Hers exceed!
Fair Trees! where s'eer your barkes I wound,
No Name shall but your own be found.

When we have run our Passions heat,
Love hither makes his best retreat.
The *Gods,* that mortal Beauty chase,
Still in a Tree did end their race.
Apollo hunted *Daphne* so,
Only that She might Laurel grow.
And *Pan* did after *Syrinx* speed,
Not as a Nymph, but for a Reed.

MICK HALES

Roses, delphiniums, irises, and poppies
Philadelphia, Pennsylvania

Hosta plantaginea and lilac bushes
(*Syringa vulgaris*)
Near Minneapolis, Minnesota

What wond'rous Life is this I lead!
Ripe Apples drop about my head;
The Luscious Clusters of the Vine
Upon my Mouth do crush their Wine;
The Nectaren and curious Peach,
Into my hands themselves do reach;
Stumbling on Melons, as I pass,
Insnar'd with Flow'rs, I fall on Grass.

Mean while the Mind, from pleasure less,
Withdraws into its happiness:
The Mind, that Ocean where each kind
Does streight its own resemblance find;
Yet it creates, transcending these,
Far other Worlds, and other Seas;
Annihilating all that's made
To a green Thought in a green Shade.

Here at the Fountains sliding foot,
Or at some Fruit-trees mossy root,
Casting the Bodies Vest aside,
My Soul into the boughs does glide:
There like a Bird it sits, and sings,
The whets, and combs its silver Wings;
And, till prepar'd for longer flight,
Waves in its Plumes the various Light.

Such was that happy Garden-state,
While Man there walk'd without a Mate:
After a Place so pure, and sweet,
What other Help could yet be meet!
But 'twas beyond a Mortal's share
To wander solitary there:
Two Paradises 'twere in one
To live in Paradise alone.

How well the skilful Gardner drew
Of flow'rs and herbes this Dial new!
Where from above the milder Sun
Does through a fragrant Zodiack run;
And, as it works, th'industrious Bee
Computes its time as well as we.
How could such sweet and wholsome Hours
Be reckon'd but with herbs and flow'rs!

SUN-DIAL INSCRIPTIONS

HASTE, TRAVELLER, ON THY WAY,
THE SUN IS SINKING LOW.
HE SHALL RETURN AGAIN,
BUT NEVER THOU.

THE SHADOW PASSES;
LIGHT REMAINS.

A CLOCK THE TIME MAY WRONGLY TELL;
I, NEVER, IF THE SUN SHINE WELL.

AS TIME AND HOURS DO PASS AWAY
SO DOTH THE LIFE OF MAN DECAY.

BE THE DAY WEARY,
BE THE DAY LONG,
SOON IT RINGS
TO EVEN SONG.

AS TIME DOTH HASTE,
SO LIFE DOTH WASTE.

LIGHT RULES ME
THE SHADOW THEE.

AMIDDST YE FLOWRES
I TELL YE HOWRES.
TIME WANES AWAYE
AS FLOWRES DECAYE.

A MOMENT—MARK HOW SMALL A SPACE
THE DIAL SHOWS UPON THE FACE;
YET WASTE BUT ONE—AND YOU WILL SEE
OF HOW GREAT MOMENT IT CAN BE.

MICK HALES

Sundial with box hedge at
Wing Haven Gardens
Charlotte, North Carolina

MICK HALES

Garden of Roberto Burle Marx
Near Rio de Janiero, Brazil

NIGHT

ELEANOR PERENYI

S cents are stronger at night. Everybody knows that but not that they are also different. Faint whiffs of sweetness in nicotiana and clethra acquire a dose of pepper after midnight—when, on the other hand, the carnations, at their most powerful at dusk, seem to go to sleep and stop smelling. But the biggest change is that of proportion and texture produced by seeing things in black and white. My first experience of this phenomenon wasn't in a garden, or at night, but in Rome in broad daylight, in the company of a friend who is color-blind. I had always known this about him and never grasped the significance until the day I stupidly said something about the apricot glow of Roman palaces. 'You forget,' he said gently, 'I don't see that. I don't know what you mean.' The words were more than an embarrassment, they were a revelation, for he was the subtlest of observers, who had often pointed out to me details and refinements in paintings and architecture, and even plants, which—blinded in my own way by color—I had missed. Thereafter, I observed things with different and in some ways better-informed eyes, and I haven't forgotten the lesson.

To see things in black and white is to see the basics, and I would now recommend to any designer of gardens that he go out and look at his work by the light of the moon. He may well see that a certain bush is too large for the space it occupies, another too small, that the placement of a flower bed needs adjusting. Above all, he will be more conscious of the importance of form. Strolling among the ruins on the Palatine, my color-blind friend had again and again identified the wild flowers growing there by their shapes, pointing out to me especially the beauty of the acanthus, so loved by the Greeks they made it the capital of the Corinthian order, and reminding me that Pliny made beds of acanthus alone, not for the flowers but for the leaves.

The Impressionists saw nature as color swimming in light, but in most of the world's great gardens color has counted for very little. Masses of brilliant shrubs and flowers are a modern idea and not necessarily a good one. Subtract the color from a garden and it can prove to be an ill-planned scramble. One way to find out is to walk around it on a summer night. But not, please, with the aid of floodlights. No matter how skillfully carried out, I abhor the introduction of electricity into a garden. Lighted pools, false dawns among the shrubs are to me both ugly and vulgar. (No, I don't like *son et lumière* either: The Parthenon bathed in lavender is a horrid sight.) A path or driveway may need to be discreetly lighted to keep people from breaking their necks, and hurricane lamps on a terrace where one is dining are more than permissible. I love an old-fashioned Japanese paper lantern stuck with a candle and hung in a tree like a moon. A spotlight trained on a fountain, no. A garden at night should be itself—a place at rest, a haven for creatures, and for me too when I want to lie in the hammock in the dark.

—FROM *GREEN THOUGHTS*

HARRY
HARALAMBOU

'Enchantment' lilies
Peconic, New York

THE GARDEN OF LIVE FLOWERS

LEWIS CARROLL

I should see the garden far better," said Alice to herself, "if I could get to the top of that hill: and here's a path that leads straight to it—at least, no, it doesn't do *that*—" (after going a few yards along the path, and turning several sharp corners), "but I suppose it will at last. But how curiously it twists! It's more like a corkscrew than a path! Well, *this* turn goes to the hill, I suppose—no, it doesn't! This goes straight back to the house! Well then, I'll try it the other way."

And so she did: wandering up and down, and trying turn after turn, but always coming back to the house, do what she would. Indeed, once, when she turned a corner rather more quickly than usual, she ran against it before she could stop herself.

"It's no use talking about it," Alice said, looking up at the house and pretending it was arguing with her. "I'm *not* going in again yet. I know I should have to get through the Looking-glass again—back into the old room—and there'd be an end of all my adventures!"

So, resolutely turning her back upon the house, she set out once more down the path, determined to keep straight on till she got to the hill. For a few minutes all went on well, and she was just saying "I really *shall* do it this time—" when the path gave a sudden twist and shook itself (as she described it afterwards), and the next moment she found herself actually walking in at the door.

"Oh, it's too bad!" she cried. "I never saw such a house for getting in the way! Never!"

However, there was the hill full in sight, so there was nothing to be done but start again. This time she came upon a large flower-bed, with a border of daisies, and a willow-tree growing in the middle.

"O Tiger-lily!" said Alice, addressing herself to one that was waving gracefully about in the wind, "I *wish* you could talk!"

"We *can* talk," said the Tiger-lily, "when there's anybody worth talking to."

Alice was so astonished that she couldn't speak for a minute: it quite seemed to take her breath away. At length, as the Tiger-lily only went on waving about, she spoke again, in a timid voice—almost in a whisper. "And can *all* the flowers talk?"

"As well as *you* can," said the Tiger-lily. "And a great deal louder."

"It isn't manners for us to begin, you know," said the Rose, "and I really was wondering when you'd speak! Said I to myself, 'Her face has got *some* sense in it, though it's not a clever one!' Still, you're the right colour, and that goes a long way."

"I don't care about the colour," the Tiger-lily remarked. "If only her petals curled up a little more, she'd be all right."

Alice didn't like being criticized, so she began asking questions. "Aren't you sometimes frightened at being planted out here, with nobody to take care of you?"

"There's the tree in the middle," said the

Rose. "What else is it good for?"

"But what could it do, if any danger came?" Alice asked.

"It could bark," said the Rose.

"It says Bough-wough!" cried a Daisy. "That's why its branches are called boughs!"

"Didn't you know *that?*" cried another Daisy. And here they all began shouting together, till the air seemed quite full of little shrill voices. "Silence, every one of you!" cried the Tiger-lily, waving itself passionately from side to side, and trembling with excitement. "They know I can't get at them!" it panted, bending its quivering head towards Alice, "or they wouldn't dare to do it!"

"Never mind!" Alice said in a soothing tone, and, stooping down to the daisies, who were just beginning again, she whispered "If you don't hold your tongues, I'll pick you!"

There was silence in a moment, and several of the pink daisies turned white.

"That's right!" said the Tiger-lily. "The daisies are the worst of all. When one speaks, they all begin together, and it's enough to make one wither to hear how they go on!"

"How is it you can all talk so nicely?" Alice said, hoping to get it into a better temper by a compliment. "I've been in many gardens before, but none of the flowers could talk."

"Put your hand down, and feel the ground," said the Tiger-lily. "Then you'll know why."

Alice did so. "It's very hard," she said; "but I don't see what that has to do with it."

"In most gardens," the Tiger-lily said, "they make the beds too soft—so that the flowers are always asleep."

This sounded a very good reason, and Alice

was quite pleased to know it. "I never thought of that before!" she said.

"It's *my* opinion that you never think *at all,*" the Rose said, in a rather severe tone.

"I never saw anybody that looked stupider," a Violet said, so suddenly, that Alice quite jumped; for it hadn't spoken before.

"Hold *your* tongue!" cried the Tiger-lily. "As if *you* ever saw anybody! You keep your head under the leaves, and snore away there, till you know no more what's going on in the world, than if you were a bud!"

"Are there any more people in the garden besides me?" Alice said, not choosing to notice the Rose's last remark.

"There's one other flower in the garden that can move about like you," said the Rose. "I wonder how you do it—" ("You're always wondering," said the Tiger-lily), "but she's more bushy than you are."

"Is she like me?" Alice asked eagerly, for the thought crossed her mind, "There's another little girl in the garden somewhere!"

"Well, she has the same awkward shape as you," the Rose said: "but she's redder—and her petals are shorter, I think."

"They're done up close, like a dahlia," said the Tiger-lily: "not tumbled about, like yours."

"But that's not *your* fault," the Rose added kindly. "You're beginning to fade, you know— and then one can't help one's petals getting a little untidy."

Alice didn't like this idea at all: so, to change the subject, she asked, "Does she ever come out here?"

"I daresay you'll see her soon," said the Rose. "She's one of the kind that has nine spikes, you know."

"Where does she wear them?" Alice asked with some curiosity.

"Why all round her head, of course," the Rose replied. "I was wondering *you* hadn't got some too. I thought it was the regular rule."

"She's coming!" cried the Larkspur. "I hear her footstep, thump, thump, along the gravel walk."

Alice looked round eagerly and found that it was the Red Queen. "She's grown a good deal!" was her first remark. She had indeed: when Alice first found her in the ashes, she had been only three inches high—and here she was, half a head taller than Alice herself!

"It's the fresh air that does it," said the Rose: "wonderfully fine air it is, out here."

"I think I'll go and meet her," said Alice, for, though the flowers were interesting enough, she felt that it would be far grander to have a talk with a real Queen.

—FROM *THROUGH THE LOOKING-GLASS*

MICK HALES

Shakespeare Garden in Central Park
New York, New York

LINES TO A NASTURTIUM

(A LOVER MUSES)

ANNE SPENCER

Flame-flower, Day-torch, Mauna Loa,
I saw a daring bee, today, pause, and soar,
        Into your flaming heart;
Then did I hear crisp, crinkled laughter
As the furies after tore him apart?
        A bird, next, small and humming,
Looked into your startled depths and fled . . . .
Surely, some dread sight, and dafter
        Than human eyes as mine can see,
Set the stricken air waves drumming
        In his flight.

Day-torch, Flame-flower, cool-hot Beauty,
I cannot see, I cannot hear your flutey
Voice lure your loving swain,
But I know one other to whom you are in beauty
Born in vain:
Hair like the setting sun,
Her eyes a rising star,
Motions gracious as reeds by Babylon, bar
All your competing;
Hands like, how like, brown lilies sweet,
Cloth of gold were fair enough to touch her feet . . .
Ah, how the sense reels at my repeating,
As once in her fire-lit heart I felt the furies
Beating, beating.

PING
AMRANAND

Nasturtiums at Brookside Gardens
Wheaton, Maryland

106

WHAT THE HERB GARDEN HAS MEANT TO ME

HELEN MORGANTHAU FOX

Herb gardening has been compared to chamber music. Both are best appreciated in small places, for they have an intimate quality lost in a large hall or in a big garden. Gardening with herbs, which is becoming increasingly popular, is indulged in by those who like subtlety in their plants in preference to brilliance.

—FROM *THE YEARS IN MY HERB GARDEN*

PING
AMRANAND

Herb Garden at Oatlands
Leesburg, Virginia

PING
AMRANAND

Lavender fields
Provence, France

LAVENDERS AND ROSEMARY

HELEN MORGANTHAU FOX

Rosemary and lavender grow wild along the shores of the Mediterranean. When one goes for a walk beside the sea in southern France in what is called the Maquis, the plants are so thick one steps on them and causes them to give forth their delicious fragrance. Voyagers to Spain since Roman days have said that the fragrance of the plants could be smelled far out to sea, and I can verify this from personal experience. There, too, trunks of large old plants are burned for firewood and send their perfume into the air through the chimneys. High up in the Spanish Sierras incense is made by burning cistus, rosemary and lavender in pits.

—FROM *THE YEARS IN MY HERB GARDEN*

HOW LILLIES CAME WHITE

ROBERT HERRICK

White though ye be; yet, Lillies, know,
From the first ye were not so:
    But Ile tell ye
    What befell ye;
Cupid and his Mother lay
In a Cloud; while both did play,
He with his pretty finger prest
The rubie niplet of her breast;
Out of the which, the creame of light,
    Like to a Dew,
    Fell downe on you,
    And made ye white.

KEN DRUSE

Giant lily (*Cardiocrinum giganteum*)
Near Philadelphia, Pennsylvania

P E T E R   M A R G O N E L L I

Giant Pacific delphiniums (*Delphinium elatum*)
Chester County, Pennsylvania

E D W A R D   S T E I C H E N

In 1929, I acquired a farm in Redding, Connecticut. From the weekends and holidays spent there, came a stream of photographs that were a vital expression of the earth… The photographs I made in the country, as well as the crossbreeding and growing of delphinium and other flowering plants, kept me in contact with nature and kept my hands in contact with the soil. Without this sustenance, I don't believe I could have remained alive and interested in my professional photographic activities in New York as long as I did.

—FROM *STEICHEN: A LIFE IN PHOTOGRAPHY*

A MARIGOLD FROM NORTH VIETNAM

─────────────────────────

FOR BARBARA DEMING

D E N I S E   L E V E R T O V

Marigold   resurrection flower
that the dead   love and come forth
by candlelight to inhale
scent of   sharp   a smoke-of-watchfires
odor.   The living
taste it as if   on the tongue
acrid.   In summer it tells   of fall
in fall   of winter   in winter
of spring.   The leaves
very fine   delicate.   The flowers
petal-crowded   long-lasting.
Drooping in dryness   the whole plant
in minutes   lifts itself   resilient
given water.   The earth in the pot was dug
in quick kindness   by moonlight   for gift
in Maine   but to the root-threads cling still
some crumbs of Vietnam.   When I water
the marigold these too   are moistened
and give forth   nourishment.

P I N G
A M R A N A N D

Flower market
Paris, France

IN A JAPANESE GARDEN

LAFCADIO HEARN

In order to comprehend the beauty of a Japanese garden, it is necessary to understand—or at least to learn to understand—the beauty of stones. Not of stones quarried by the hand of man, but of stones shaped by nature only. Until you can feel, and keenly feel, that stones have character, that stones have tones and values, the whole artistic meaning of a Japanese garden cannot be revealed to you. . . . At the approaches to temples, by the side of roads, before holy groves, and in all parks and pleasure-grounds, as well as in all cemeteries, you will notice large, irregular, flat slabs of natural rock—mostly from the river beds and water-worn—sculptured with ideographs, but unhewn. These have been set up as votive tablets, as commemorative monuments, as tombstones, and are much more costly than the ordinary cut-stone columns and haka chiseled with the figures of divinities in relief. Again, you will see before most of the shrines, nay, even in the grounds of nearly all large homesteads, great irregular blocks of granite or other hard rock, worn by the action of torrents, and converted into water-basins (*chodzubachi*) by cutting a circular hollow in the top. Such are but common examples of the utilization of stones even in the poorest villages; and if you have any natural artistic sentiment, you cannot fail to discover, sooner or later, how much more beautiful are these natural forms than any shapes from the hand of the stone-cutter.

—FROM *GLIMPSES OF UNFAMILIAR JAPAN*

PING
AMRANAND

Garden at Nanzen-ji
Kyoto, Japan

EXCLUSIVE BLUE

ROBERT FRANCIS

Her flowers were exclusive blue.
No other color scheme would do.

Better than God she could reject
Being a gardener more select.

Blue, blue it was against the green
With nothing *not* blue sown or seen.

Yet secretly she half-confessed
With blue she was not wholly blessed.

All blues, she found, do not agree.
Blue riots in variety.

Purist-perfectionist at heart,
Her vision flew beyond her art—

Beyond her art, her touch, her power
To teach one blue to each blue flower.

KEN DRUSE

Hydrangea macrophylla 'Blue Wave'
Brooklyn, New York

KEN DRUSE

Salvia × superba 'East Freisland',
Salvia Sclarea 'Clary Sage',
daisies, and astilbes
Bucks County, Pennsylvania

CURTICE
TAYLOR

White lotus at Innisfree Garden
Millbrook, New York

THE ORNAMENTATION OF PONDS AND LAKES

SAMUEL PARSONS, JR.

The lotus leaves and flowers are decorative and striking in effect, but the true water-lilies, the *Nymphaeas*, are, after all, I am inclined to say, the best ornamental water-plants. Following out my Lombardy poplar idea of emphasis, I used many lotuses in front of my brook and pond promontories. But in all my experiments with aquatic plants I never chanced on any pond-effects quite equal to that of my coves of *Nymphaeas* in midsummer. Fancy a quiet, mirror-like surface of water, studded with clustering masses of lily-pads,

118

enfolding half-open flowers, nestling, yet buoyant. Every one is familiar with scenes in woodland nooks resembling this in kind. The remarkable difference on my place was that my trees and shrubs, grasses and flowers, came to the water's edge and were mirrored there, and that in front and about them floated and were reflected lily-pads of excellent size and coloring. The flowers also of these great tropical lilies were especially large and richly hued, some species being pure white, others red, and still others purple and deep blue. I have had these water-lilies and other water-plants growing on my place now for several years, but I confess that, even at the present time, familiar as they are to me, when I look at one of these blue lilies on an early summer morning I am impressed with the scene as an absolute revelation of beauty, a landscape feature positively unique.

—FROM *LANDSCAPE GARDENING*

CURTICE
TAYLOR

Water lilies including the giant
Victoria regia at Longwood Gardens
Kennett Square, Pennsylvania

MICK HALES

Ornamental grasses including
Miscanthus sinensis and
Calamagrostis × *acutiflora stricta* at
Stonecrop Gardens
Cold Spring, New York

A WHITE-PAPER GARDEN

SARA ANDREW SHAFER

I should like to have a grass garden. Think of the possibilities of a stretch of ground given over to it, and to whatever else the wind cared to add to it by way of seedlings. The gentle little silvery grass just spoken of should be there; the aristocratic blue grass—the tall, soldierly timothy, with its purple-fringed banners; the redtop in which one sees a forecast of oak-woods in autumn; the foxtails; the quaking grasses, and many another whose names I do not know, but of whose beauties I am sure. To be perfect, this garden would slope downward to a marshy hollow, where wild rice and many sedges would grow, and should rise to a hill-crest down which winds should race over billowing, golden wheat, or grey-green oats. Maize would be planted in a field so close at hand that all the summer would be filled with the music of its leaves, whisper, whisper, whispering; and somewhere about should be a patch of broom corn and of sorghum to show how regal are the growths of these largest grasses of the temperate zone. Of grasses alone a most lovely garden could be made, but among them what a succession of other things would give themselves permission to grow! Dandelions would be almost the first comers, unbuttoning their flat rosettes of dented leaves from the sod, and throwing out a few coins of that larger minting which is the true largesse of May. Clovers would follow, daisies would follow. Buttercups would be there, bindweeds, milkweeds, speedwell, catchfly, yarrow, with mullein, mints, each so generously given, each stealing after his forerunner so silently and so surely that we have hardly time to say "The clover is here," before the clover has gone, and we are crying "It is yarrow-day!"

—FROM *A White-Paper Garden*

The clear afternoon was drowsy and sad,
a summer afternoon. Ivy strands dangled
dusty and black, from the garden wall …
        A fountain was splashing.
        With a grating noise my key turned the lock.
The rusty old gate on its strident hinge
slowly gave way, then swung heavily to
and struck the silence of the dead afternoon.
        Through the empty garden the gurgling sound
of the water singing its run-on lines
led me to the fountain. The fountain was dripping
monotony down on the white marble slab.
        The fountain sang: "Does it all come back,
the faraway dream, on my present song?
The slow afternoon in the summer's slow time… "
        I answered the fountain:
"It does not come back
but your singing, I know, has a faraway sound."
        "This was the very afternoon. Just as now
my water streamed down
and spread its monotony over the marble.
Don't you remember? These long-cassocked myrtles
you see now were shading clear songs
you now hear. Ripe flame-colored fruit
hung down from the branch
as it hangs today. Don't you remember?…
It was this same slow summer afternoon."
        "These faraway daydreams—what can they be,
that your laughing verse keeps recalling to me?
        I know your bright water with its joyous sound
once tasted the flame-colored fruit of the tree,
and I know my bitterness is a distant thing
dreaming the old summer afternoon away.

HARRY
HARALAMBOU

Water garden at the Generalife
Granada, Spain

123

I know your mirrors as they sang their song
reflected raptures of yesterday's love
but tell me, fountain of enchanted tongue,
my happy legend forgotten so long."

"I have no joyous old legends to tell:
old melancholy times are all I recall.

One bright afternoon in the summer's slow time …
alone with your suffering you sought out my rhyme.
Your lips pressed down to my tranquil flow;
in the bright afternoon they related your woe.

Your burning lips related your pain.
Thirsty they were then, thirsty they remain."

"Goodbye forever, fountain of song,
the sleepy old garden's eternal tongue.
Goodbye forever—your monotone
is bitterer far than this pain of my own."

With a grating noise my key turned the lock.
The rusty old gate on its strident hinge
slowly gave way, then swung heavily to
and rang through the silence of the dead afternoon.

CURTICE
TAYLOR

View from the Generalife toward
the Alhambra
Granada, Spain

124

THE GENERALIFE

WASHINGTON IRVING

High above the Alhambra, on the breast of the mountain, amidst embowered gardens and stately terraces, rise the lofty towers and white walls of the Generalife; a fairy palace, full of storied recollections. Here are still to be seen the famous cypresses of enormous size which flourished in the time of the Moors, and which tradition has connected with the fabulous story of Boabdil and his Sultana.

Here are preserved the portraits of many who figured in the romantic drama of the Conquest. Ferdinand and Isabella, Ponce de Leon, the gallant Marquis of Cadiz, and Garcilaso de la Vega, who slew in desperate fight Tarfe the Moor, a champion of Herculean strength. Here too hangs a portrait which has long passed for that of the unfortunate Boabdil, but which is said to be that of Aben Hud, the Moorish king from whom descended the princes of Almeria. From one of these princes, who joined the standard of Ferdinand and Isabella towards the close of the Conquest, and was Christianized by the name of Don Pedro de Granada Venegas, was descended the present proprietor of the palace, the Marquis of Campotejar. The proprietor, however, dwells in a foreign land, and the palace has no longer a princely inhabitant.

Yet here is everything to delight a southern voluptuary: fruits, flowers, fragrance, green arbors and myrtle hedges, delicate air and gushing waters. Here I had an opportunity of witnessing those scenes which painters are fond of depicting about southern palaces and gardens. It was the saint's day of the count's daughter, and she had brought up several of her youthful companions from Granada, to sport away a long summer's day among the breezy halls and bowers of the Moorish palaces. A visit to the Generalife was the morning's entertainment. Here some of the gay company dispersed itself in groups about the green walks, the bright fountains, the flights of Italian steps, the noble terraces and marble balustrades. Others, among whom I was one, took their seats in an open gallery or colonnade commanding a vast prospect; with the Alhambra, the city, and the Vega, far below, and the distant horizon of mountains—a dreamy world, all glimmering to the eye in summer sunshine. While thus seated, the all-pervading tinkling of the guitar and click of the castanets came stealing up from the valley of the Darro, and half-way down the mountain we descried a festive party under the trees, enjoying themselves in true Andalusian style; some lying on the grass, others dancing to the music.

—FROM *THE ALHAMBRA*

In a fantastic light:
blue of hydrangeas, white
and pink. That light

before the evening starts
to come fast. The sweet smell
of rye and grasses, the

sounds of animals from
the barns, red, of course,
the hand up against

light touching the blossom.
Blue. It must be blue, the
other hand falling

away in casual gesture.
Innocent. The fantastic light.
Caught. Stiff. Concrete.

PING
AMRANAND

Blue hydrangeas
Charleston, South Carolina

126

RICHARD
FELBER

Cosmos, zinnias, coreopsis, spider
plants, balloon flowers, black-eyed
Susans, and marigolds
Kent, Connecticut

THE COSMOS FLOWER

WAKAYAMA KISHI-KO

Oh, that I,
   In my demeanour,
Might be like the modest single-petalled
   Cosmos flower!

G A R D E N   V A R I E T Y

S U Z A N N A H   L E S S A R D

A friend of ours has become preoccupied with people and their gardens. She is not particularly interested in gardening herself, but she is surrounded by people who are, and the differences in their style have become for her a focus of contemplation. For example, her father's garden—vegetables, with flowers around the borders—is stunningly tidy. Each type of vegetable grows in a perfect straight row. The tomatoes—several varieties (including the Early Girl, which begins to yield around the middle of July), to insure a steady supply over a long period—are tied to symmetrical wooden frames. There is not a weed in sight. Her father's garden also happens to be situated on a slope, and he has built terraces, with walls of smooth white rocks, in size somewhere between a stone and a boulder, which are to be found on the beaches of the North Shore of Long Island. Since storms move the rocks up and down the beach quite a lot, this project often entailed lugging them a long way to the car before carrying them up the steep hill on which his house is built. The terracing was not absolutely necessary, although it does help the soil to retain moisture. The rocks were certainly not necessary in order to terrace the garden, although the job is better with them than it would be without, and their sea-blanched color has a startling, incongruous beauty in this green setting. In admiring his handiwork, our friend remarked to her father that his garden

was like an Italian one, whereupon he looked a little affronted and said he had thought of it as like New England. The daughter does not recall having seen many terraced gardens in New England, but that hardly matters. Her father is dissatisfied with his house, because it is near a noisy road, and he plans to move when he can find a better one, but he hopes that the owner who comes after him will enjoy the terraces.

Then our friend considers her mother's garden. It lies on flat ground and merges in an indefinite way with the lawn, which has both inroads and independent satellites within the garden. Her mother does not like rows, or the segregation of different kinds of vegetables, or even the broader distinctions between herbs, flowers, and vegetables. Pepper grows next to eggplant, and has a brother beyond a swatch of parsley, and another pleasantly consorting with a congregation of onions. Her mother says that the Italians plant their gardens this way. The daughter, who has been to Italy several times but admits that she does not know that country as intimately as her mother does, came away with a rather different impression. The Italian question is moot, however, for while it is possible that some Florentines or Neapolitans plant gardens in a design like that of a patchwork quilt, the domination in this garden of huge, unruly presences removes it absolutely from that theory of design. There is, for example, a multi-

H U G H
P A L M E R

Varieties of lettuce at Hunstrete House
Somerset, England

MICK HALES

Roses and vegetables at
Barnsley House
Gloucestershire, England

130

ple and anarchic tomato plant that sprang to life by itself in the wheelbarrow this spring and now sprawls over the garden bearing three or four extremely unpromising hard, yellowish fruits. Also, there is a roving squash plant that was found in the brush dump on the edge of the property and has produced a profusion of fruits of a pale-green hue, with subtle, elaborate markings (quite unlike any other squash witnesses have ever seen), and many luminous golden flowers, one of which grows at the very end of a particularly adventurous runner that has found its way out of the garden and several feet into the lawn proper, thereby destroying whatever semblance of a boundary might have existed before. The daughter privately believes that this garden is without precedent, but she holds her tongue. This is partly because, near the front walk, a mob of bushy and towering black-eyed Susans, noble savages that loudly announce the presence of the garden (which an inattentive passerby might not recognize and therefore might clumsily damage), stare down, with innocent righteousness, any critical observer.

These two gardeners are divorced.

Our friend has tried to come to terms with the two gardens by reaching for conceptual definitions: classicism versus romanticism, for example, or reason versus intuition. She wonders what sort of garden she, the child of such willful, antipodal agriculturists, would herself create, and definitions like these offer a flimsy hope of resolving this crisis of identity. However, none of these abstract ideas hold up very well when she includes one other garden in her inquiry. That is her maternal grandmother's garden. Flowers, primarily large, spectacular roses, grow there, as do vegetables and herbs. The different kinds of plants are not all mixed up but neither are they clearly segregated; they grow in groups together. A first impression of this garden is of lushness and joyous abandon—of a romantic, intuitive creation, almost overgrown—but on closer inspection a firm underlying order becomes evident: the ground is mulched; the tall plants are staked; the roses, exuberant as they are, show signs of pruning; and the flagstone path down the middle to a white iron bench beneath an arbor of wild grapes, while intruded upon by the garden, has nevertheless been kept just barely passable. The dynamic combination of order and anarchy which constitutes the character of this garden is summed up, perhaps, by a remark our friend's grandmother once made upon learning, to her horror, that her daughter—the whimsical gardener, next door—did not own a functioning clock. "If you will not accept a clock from me," she said after several offers had been refused, "I shall blow up your house."

ODE TO THE ONION

PABLO NERUDA

Onion,
shining flask,
your beauty assembled
petal by petal,
they affixed crystal scales to you
and your belly of dew grew round
in the secret depth of the dark earth.
The miracle took place
underground,
and when your lazy green stalk
appeared
and your leaves were born
like swords in the garden,
the earth gathered its strength
exhibiting your naked transparency,
and just as the distant sea
copied the magnolia in Aphrodite
raising up her breasts,
so the earth
made you,
onion,
as clear as a planet
and fated
to shine,
constant constellation,
rounded rose of water,
on
poor people's
dining tables.

Generously
you give up
your balloon of freshness
to the boiling consummation

of the pot,
and in the blazing heat of the oil
the shred of crystal
is transformed into a curled feather of gold.

I shall also proclaim how your influence
livens the salad's love,
and the sky seems to contribute
giving you the fine shape of hail
praising your chopped brightness
upon the halves of a tomato.
But within the people's reach,
showered with oil,
dusted
with a pinch of salt,
you satisfy the worker's hunger
along the hard road home.
Poor people's star,
fairy godmother
wrapped
in fancy paper, you rise from the soil,
eternal, intact, as pure
as a celestial body,
and when the kitchen knife
cuts you
the only painless tear
is shed:
you made us weep without suffering.
I have praised every living thing, onion,
but for me you are
more beautiful than a bird
of blinding plumage;
to my eyes you are
a heavenly balloon, platinum cup,
the snowy anemone's
motionless dance.
The fragrance of the earth is alive
in your crystalline nature.

—FROM *ODAS ELEMENTALES*

MICK HALES

Farmer's garden
Zelum, China

WHAT I KNOW ABOUT GARDENING

CHARLES DUDLEY WARNER

The principal value of a private garden is not understood. It is not to give the possessor vegetables and fruit (that can be better and cheaper done by market-gardeners), but to teach him patience and philosophy, and the higher virtues,—hope deferred, and expectations blighted, leading directly to resignation, and sometimes to alienation. The garden thus becomes a moral agent, a test of character, as it was in the beginning. I shall keep this central truth in mind in these articles. I mean to have a moral garden, if it is not a productive one,—one that shall teach, O my brothers! O my sisters! the great lessons of life.

The first pleasant thing about a garden in this latitude is, that you never know when to set it going. If you want any thing to come to maturity early, you must start it in a hot-house. If you put it out early, the chances are all in favor of getting it nipped with frost; for the thermometer will be 90° one day, and go below 32° the night of the day following. And, if you do not set out plants or sow seeds early, you fret continually; knowing that your vegetables will be late, and that, while Jones has early peas, you will be watching your slow-forming pods. This keeps you in a state of mind. When you have planted any thing early, you are doubtful whether to desire to see it above ground, or not. If a hot day comes, you long to see the young plants; but, when a cold north wind brings frost, you tremble lest the seeds have burst their bands. Your spring is passed in anxious doubts and fears, which are usually realized; and so a great moral discipline is worked out for you.

—FROM *My Summer in a Garden*

THE ROUND

STANLEY KUNITZ

Light splashed this morning
on the shell-pink anemones
swaying on their tall stems;
down blue-spiked veronica
light flowed in rivulets
over the humps of the honeybees;
this morning I saw light kiss
the silk of the roses
in their second flowering,
my late bloomers
flushed with their brandy.
A curious gladness shook me.

So I have shut the doors of my house,
so I have trudged downstairs to my cell,
so I am sitting in semi-dark
hunched over my desk
with nothing for a view
to tempt me
but a bloated compost heap,
steamy old stinkpile,
under my window;
and I pick my notebook up
and I start to read aloud
the still-wet words I scribbled
on the blotted page:
"Light splashed . . ."

I can scarcely wait till tomorrow
when a new life begins for me,
as it does each day,
as it does each day.

CURTICE
TAYLOR

Dahlias in the garden of
Stanley Kunitz
Provincetown, Massachusetts

136

QUEEN-ANNE'S-LACE

WILLIAM CARLOS WILLIAMS

Her body is not so white as
anemone petals nor so smooth—nor
so remote a thing. It is a field
of the wild carrot taking
the field by force; the grass
does not raise above it.
Here is no question of whiteness,
white as can be, with a purple mole
at the center of each flower.
Each flower is a hand's span
of her whiteness. Wherever
his hand has lain there is
a tiny purple blemish. Each part
is a blossom under his touch
to which the fibres of her being
stem one by one, each to its end,
until the whole field is a
white desire, empty, a single stem,
a cluster, flower by flower,
a pious wish to whiteness gone over—
or nothing.

RICHARD
FELBER

Field of Queen-Anne's-lace
Wassic, New York

HUGH
PALMER

Vegetables at Peper Harrow
Surrey, England

138

T H E   O L D   M A N S E

N A T H A N I E L   H A W T H O R N E

Childless men, if they would know something of the bliss of paternity, should plant a seed,—be it squash, bean, Indian corn, or perhaps a mere flower or worthless weed,—should plant it with their own hands, and nurse it from infancy to maturity altogether by their own care. If there be not too many of them, each individual plant becomes an object of separate interest. My garden, that skirted the avenue of the Manse, was of precisely the right extent. An hour or two of morning labor was all that it required. But I used to visit and revisit it a dozen times a day, and stand in deep contemplation over my vegetable progeny with a love that nobody could share or conceive of who had never taken part in the process of creation. It was one of the most bewitching sights in the world to observe a hill of beans thrusting aside the soil, or a row of early peas just peeping forth sufficiently to trace a line of delicate green. Later in the season the humming-birds were attracted by the blossoms of a peculiar variety of bean; and they were a joy to me, those little spiritual visitants, for deigning to sip airy food out of my nectar cups. Multitudes of bees used to bury themselves in the yellow blossoms of the summer squashes. This, too, was a deep satisfaction; although when they had laden themselves with sweets they flew away to some unknown hive, which would give back nothing in requittal of what my garden had contributed. But I was glad thus to fling a benefaction upon the passing breeze with the certainty that somebody must profit by it, and that there would be a little more honey in the world to allay the sourness and bitterness which mankind is always complaining of. Yes, indeed; my life was the sweeter for that honey.

Speaking of summer squashes, I must say a word of their beautiful and varied forms. They presented an endless diversity of urns and vases, shallow or deep, scalloped or plain, moulded in patterns which a sculptor would do well to copy, since Art has never invented anything more graceful. A hundred squashes in the garden were worthy, in my eyes at least, of being rendered indestructible in marble. If ever Providence (but I know it never will) should assign me a superfluity of gold, part of it shall be expended for a service of plate, or most delicate porcelain, to be wrought into the shapes of summer squashes gathered from vines which I will plant with my own hands. As dishes for containing vegetables they would be peculiarly appropriate.

But not merely the squeamish love of the beautiful was gratified by my toil in the kitchen garden. There was a hearty enjoyment, likewise, in observing the growth of the crook-necked winter squashes, from the first little bulb, with the withered blossom adhering to it, until they lay strewn upon the soil, big, round fellows, hiding their heads beneath the leaves, but turning up their great yellow rotundities to the noontide sun. Gazing at them, I felt that by my agency something worth living for had been done. A new substance was born in to the world. They were real and tangible existences, which the mind could seize hold of and rejoice in. A cabbage, too,—especially the early Dutch cabbage, which swells to a monstrous circumference, until its ambitious heart often bursts asunder,—is a matter to be proud of when we can claim a share with the earth and sky in producing it. But, after all, the hugest pleasure is reserved until these vegetable children of ours are smoking on the table, and we, like Saturn, make a meal of them.

—FROM *THE OLD MANSE*

MICK HALES

Kitchen garden at Hope End
Ledbury, England

140

THE VEGETABLE GARDENS AT BILIGNIN

ALICE B. TOKLAS

The work in the vegetables—Gertrude Stein was undertaking for the moment the care of the flowers and box hedges—was a full-time job and more. Later it became a joke, Gertrude Stein asking me what I saw when I closed my eyes, and I answered, Weeds. That, she said, was not the answer, and so weeds were changed to strawberries. The small strawberries, called by the French wood strawberries, are not wild but cultivated. It took me an hour to gather a small basket for Gertrude Stein's breakfast, and later when there was a plantation of them in the upper garden our young guests were told that if they cared to eat them they should do the picking themselves.

The first gathering of the garden in May of salads, radishes and herbs made me feel like a mother about her baby—how could anything so beautiful be mine. And this emotion of wonder filled me for each vegetable as it was gathered every year. There is nothing that is comparable to it, as satisfactory or as thrilling, as gathering the vegetables one has grown.

Later when vegetables were ready to be picked it never occurred to us to question what way to cook them. Naturally the simplest, just to steam or boil them and serve them with the excellent country butter or cream that we had from a farmer almost within calling distance. Later still, when we had guests and the vegetables had lost the aura of a new-born miracle, sauces added variety.

In the beginning it was the habit to pick all vegetables very young except beetroots, potatoes and large squash and pumpkins because of one's eagerness, and later because of their delicate flavour when cooked. That prevented serving sauces with some vegetables—green peas, string beans (indeed all peas and beans) and lettuces. There were exceptions, and for French guests this was one of them.

—FROM *THE ALICE B. TOKLAS COOK BOOK*

RICHARD
FELBER

Stand of loosestrife
Wassic, New York

142

B R O O K S   A T K I N S O N

The marshes along the river have come into their supreme glory. The purple loose-strife is in bloom. Probably it has been blossoming for two or three weeks, without being conspicuous. But now the profusion of purple spikes fills the marshes with royal color that represents the inexhaustible vitality of nature. The summer heat of the sun produces the boldest colors of the year. There are other flowers along the railroad track. The goldenrod is in its prime. Joe-Pye weed lifts its domes of crimson flowers four or five feet above the mud and rocks, swaying with terror when the heavy train rushes by. But the purple loose-strife is the king of the river swamps. It rules an extravagant empire that reaches deep into the city as far the Bronx River, and turns the Hudson Valley into a long corridor of splendor. The loose-strife blossoming in August is like a second spring. In abundance and color it is more imposing than the daintier flowers of May and June.

—FROM *ONCE AROUND THE SUN*

~~~~~~

M A B E L   O S G O O D   W R I G H T

I have realized anew the almost spiritual beauty of the common morning-glory. I avoided planting these flowers anywhere about the garden, because they seed so freely that they soon become an annoyance, strangling more important plants, and even tangling up the vegetables mischievously. Instead, I have given them a screen that breaks the bareness of the tool house, and let them run riot. The leaves are not especially notable, being rather coarse; but the flowers are as exquisite in their richly coloured fragility as if Aurora, in the bath, had amused herself by blowing bubbles. These, catching the sunrise glow, floated away upon the breeze, and falling on a wayside vine, opened into flowers that from their origin vanish again under the sun's caress.

Among all their colours none is more beautiful or usual than the rich purple with the ruddy throat merging to white—night shadows melting into the clear of dawn.

—FROM *THE GARDEN OF A COMMUTER'S WIFE*

H A R R Y
H A R A L A M B O U

Morning-glories and *Sedum*
'Autumn Joy'
Peconic, New York

145

KELMSCOTT
AUGUST 24, 1888

Dearest own Jenny

Here we have been for two days now, and I have been enjoying myself much, especially as Wednesday was a wholly beautiful day. . . .

As to the garden, it seems to me its chief fruit is—blackbirds. However, they have left us some (fruit) gooseberries, and I shall set to work this morning & get some before their next sit-down meal. As for flowers the July glory has departed, as needs must; but the garden looks pleasant though not very flowery. Those Sweet Sultans are run very much to leaf, but the beds in which they and the Scabious are look very pretty, the latter having very delicate foliage. There are too tall hollyocks (O so tall) by the strawberries, one white, one a very pretty red:

there are still a good many poppies in blossom; a bed of Chainy-oysters, and a good many scattered about; also a good few Dianthus Hedwiggii which look very pretty: few apples few plums, plenty of vegetables else.

Weather doubtful: I woke up this morning to a most splendid but very stormy sunrise. The nights have been fine, and the moon rises her old way from behind the great barn.

We have a post-card from Crom & he is coming this evening for a very brief stay. It seems quite strange to be here without you, my darling, and you may guess how much I think of you. Best love, my own,

from Your loving father
William Morris

—FROM *THE COLLECTED LETTERS
OF WILLIAM MORRIS*

PIMPING FOR A PUMPKIN

LEWIS GANNETT

Gardening can become a kind of disease. It infects you; you cannot escape from it. When you go visiting, your eyes rove about the garden; you interrupt the serious cocktail drinking by an irresistible impulse to get up and pull a weed. And Ruth and I have become such hopelessly infected gardeners that, though when in the city we live in what was once the janitor's apartment on the roof of a corset factory, even there we have a garden. It began with a wagonload of Union Square.

Mr. Moses was lifting the face of the old square and removing a good deal of its body as waste material. Egmont, my predecessor in the penthouse, arranged a private deal with a willing truckman to dump one of his loads at the freight entrance to our loft building; Egmont and the night watchman moved the rubble to the roof.

Egmont began his planting in butter tubs and wooden boxes, which promptly rotted. Ruth and I replaced them with creosote-painted boxes and conscientiously equipped them with drainage holes. Our boxes may have lasted a little longer than the uncreosoted ones, but they rotted too. So we just spread the earth on the roof between two skylights, and the garden prospered. The skylights didn't. One autumn the factory tenant beneath us complained of leakage, and we had to shovel the earth away

from the skylights and, at considerable expense, build a brick retaining wall about a more restricted roof garden.

We needed to restrict it, in any case, because our earth was washing away. We had improved the Union Square subsoil with an almost indefinite number of sacks of finely rotted humus from the Cream Hill mulch pile, but as one grows older one finds that the charm of moving hundred-pound sacks of soil tends to wane.

However, in the course of nearly twenty years of roof gardening, we discovered a lot of primary facts which do not jibe with the rosy prognostications of the garden pages, with the extravagances of the plusher penthouse-garden advertisements, or even with our Cream Hill experiences. Some of our discoveries make things easier, and some vice versa.

What we grow on the roof today is essentially a residue. We've tried a little of almost everything, mostly by accident. I have a strange passion for ferns, and have lugged in from the country an extraordinary number of cartons full of them. I prefer maidenhair, but it doesn't like the sooty city. In the city, maidenhair looks beautiful the first May and June, turns brown come midsummer, pokes its nose up bravely the second year, and never amounts to anything again. The true fiddle ferns—what filicophiles call cinnamon ferns and interrupted ferns—

148

seem actually to like the city. They do too well, in fact, the first year, and grow so tall that the wind breaks them. They tend to be a bit smaller the second year, and last for a good five or six years. Probably they would last longer still with expert attention, which ours don't get. Lady ferns prosper in spring and turn brown in midsummer, but if you cut the fronds, they come back nicely. We learned that it doesn't pay to import ferns in midsummer. The time to bring them in is when the fiddle fronds are just showing above ground. . . .

The Cream Hill season begins three weeks later than New York's, which is a disadvantage from the point of view of starting plants for city use in the country. In the course of the years we have discovered that certain plants seed themselves in the city. We never have to buy nicotiana, or marigold, or calliopsis, or sunflowers. The three or four stalks of sunflower which we allow to grow at the back of the roof garden each year would, if permitted to do so, seed a city acre. They seem to need no nourishment at all. I have found sunflowers sprouting and even,

KEN DRUSE

Rooftop garden
New York, New York

C U R T I C E
T A Y L O R

Rooftop garden
New York, New York

in a stunted way, blooming in the gravel in the gutter on the roof, which was probably enriched somewhat by the wash from our garden. Marigold and calliopsis seldom reseed themselves on Cream Hill, but each spring in the city I find several plants starting bravely under the garden litter, and they do well. Nicotiana will grow anywhere.

Petunias and zinnias don't seed themselves in the city, but they flourish. Calendulas, which sprout like weeds in our Cream Hill vegetable garden, won't grow in the city at all. For years my theory was that their sticky leaves got clogged with deposits from the city smoke, but one day a friend pointed out that the petunia leaves were sticky too and that they didn't suffer. It's another mystery.

We've tried bulbs, and they don't do badly. Every year at least one snowdrop blooms in February, which is an encouraging phenomenon. We never remember to lift tulips in summer, as the books advise, and so they peter out. So do daffodils.

We have a lawn too. It is, I think, the feature of our roof garden most admired by visitors. It is roughly ten feet long and six feet wide, and we cut it with a regular lawn mower. We used shears for years, but that's a slow job. The soil under our lawn cannot be more than three inches deep; the grass needs constant watering and also, we have discovered, a scattering of fertilizer once every month or so through the summer. But it grows. I doubt if any putting green has more cherished grass.

150

The victory-garden experts, I understand, advised against vegetable gardening on city roofs. In the general contagion of wartime, however, we couldn't avoid a few vitamin experiments. We had always had chives (it, too, seeds itself all over the roof), we've had parsley, and we brought in mint with the ferns some years ago. The mint, if encouraged, would take most of the garden. You don't need much mint, however, for an occasional julep. For reasons which the Botanical Garden could doubtless explain, our city mint gets pretty seedy before September. We have grown city radishes on occasion, simple because radishes grow quickly, and there's a time in the spring when you want something to show for your efforts.

In 1943 we succumbed to the martial atmosphere and grew a few other vegetables on the roof. We had at least one good mess of beans—I contend we had two, but Ruth doesn't remember it that way—and we had several messes of oakleaf lettuce. Also, we had tomatoes.

As a matter of fact, we had peppers too. But we didn't have eggplants. We bought three plants of tomatoes, three of peppers, and three of eggplants in May and set them in. They grew very nicely. They put out leaves and in due time put out flowers too. But the flowers wilted and dropped and there was never any suggestion of actual tomatoes or peppers. The tomato plants began to get tall, so I tied them to the trellises. The pepper plants were covered with waxy little white flowers, and the eggplants put out their sultry purple bloom. But no fruit.

It was an office associate, the garden editor of the *Herald Tribune*, who solved my problem. He was writing weekly articles explaining that one should not over-fertilize or under-fertilize, or over-water or under-water tomatoes, and I told him I'd tried all those things and none of them worked.

"Have you any bees up there?" Jack asked.

I looked that evening when I got home. We hadn't. It was, I think about the only category of insect missing. We had flies, aphids, butterflies, moths, centipedes, beetles, and ladybugs—once we had even had a grasshopper—but we had no bees.

"Well, then," Jack said the next time I saw him, "you've got to act like a bee. Pimp 'em."

He told me then the story of the man who, when his pumpkins wouldn't set, wrote to his congressman, who referred his letter to the Department of Agriculture. The Department replied, suggesting to him that perhaps his pumpkin flowers were not being properly fertilized and that, if he had no bees, he could substitute for them by brushing the pollen off some of the flowers and onto others with a camel's-hair paintbrush.

The man refused. "I grew up on a farm," he said, "and as a boy I led the stallion to the mare and the boar to the sow, but I'll be doggoned if I'll pimp for a pumpkin."

I pimped for my tomatoes. I brushed the pollen one Friday afternoon, departed for Cream Hill, and when I looked again on Monday morning I could already see the little green tomatoes forming. It was miraculous. I didn't begin pimping until mid-July, but even so we had a good tomato harvest. The peppers succumbed to my mediation too, but the eggplants refused. Apparently they insist on their own private sex life.

—FROM *CREAM HILL*

AH! SUN-FLOWER

WILLIAM BLAKE

Ah Sun-flower! Weary of time,
Who countest the steps of the Sun:
Seeking after that sweet golden clime
Where the traveller's journey is done.

Where the Youth pined away with desire,
And the pale Virgin shrouded in snow:
Arise from their graves and aspire,
Where my Sun-flower wishes to go.

PING
AMRANAND

Sunflower fields
Provence, France

A BOUQUET OF ZINNIAS

MONA VAN DUYN

One could not live without delicacy, but when
I think of love I think of the big, clumsy-looking
hands of my grandmother, each knuckle a knob,
stiff from the time it took for hard grasping,
with only my childhood's last moment for the soft touch.
And I think of love this August when I look
at the zinnias on my coffee table. Housebound
by a month-long heat wave, sick simply of summer,
nursed by the cooler's monotone of comfort,
I brought myself flowers, a sequence of multicolors.
How tough they are, how bent on holding their flagrant
freshness, how stubbornly in their last days instead
of fading they summon an even deeper hue
as if they intended to dry to everlasting,
and how suddenly, heavily, they hang their heads at the end.
A "high prole" flower, says Fussell's book on American
class, the aristocrat wouldn't touch them, says Cooper
on class in England. So unguardedly, unthriftily
do they open up and show themselves that subtlety,
rarity, nuance are almost put to shame.
Utter clarity of color, as if amidst all that
mystery inside and outside one's own skin
this at least were something unmistakable,
multiplicity of both color and form, as if
in certain parts of our personal economy
abundance were precious—these are their two main virtues.
In any careless combination they delight.

MICK HALES

Zinnias, cosmos, and sunflowers
Western Connecticut

Pure peach-cheek beside the red of a boiled beet
by the perky scarlet of a cardinal by flamingo pink
by sunsink orange by yellow from a hundred buttercups
by bleached linen white. Any random armful
of the world, one comes to feel, would fit together.
They try on petal shapes in public, from prim scallops
to coleslaw shreds of a peony heart, to the tousle
of a football chrysanthemum, to the guilelessness
of a gap-toothed daisy, and back to a welter
of stiff, curved dahlia-like quills. They all reach out.

It has been a strange month, a month of zinnias.
As any new focus of feeling makes for the mind's
refreshment (one of love's multitudinous uses),
so does a rested mind manage to modify
the innate blatancy of the heart. I have studied these blooms
who publish the fact that nothing is tentative
about love, have applauded their willingness to take
love's ultimate risk of being misapprehended.
But there are other months in the year, other levels
of inwardness, other ways of loving. In the shade
in my garden, leaf-sheltering lilies of the valley,
for instance, will keep in tiny, exquisite bells
their secret clapper. And up from my bulbs will come
welcome Dutch irises whose transcendent blue,
bruisable petals curve sweetly over their center.

KEN DRUSE

Zinnias and snapdragons at the
New York Botanical Garden
Bronx, New York

AUGUST 31

RICHARDSON WRIGHT

The warning. On these late August nights we listen carefully, like men awaiting an inevitable doom, for the music of the katydids. The date is set down and as surely as day follows night, in six weeks' time the Zinnias will curl and brown at the first touch of the White Frost and many another tender plant will shrivel in the cold that devastates our hilltop. On these first katydid nights we realize that the Summer laziness is drawing to a close: soon will come the busy Autumn.

—FROM *THE GARDENER'S BED-BOOK*

AUTUMN

HUGH
PALMER

Autumn crocuses (*Colchicum
speciosum* 'Album') at Howick Hall
Northumberland, England

FLOWERS OF MYSTERY

ALICE MORSE EARLE

The hardy Colchicum or Autumnal Crocus is seldom seen in our gardens; nor do I care for its increase, even when planted in the grass. It bears to me none of the delight which accompanies the spring Crocus, but seems to be out of keeping with the autumnal season. Rising bare of leaves, it has but a seminatural aspect, as if it had been stuck rootless in the ground like the leafless, stemless blooms of a child's posy bed. Its English name—Naked Boys—seems suited to it. The Colchicum is associated in my mind with the Indian Pipe and similar growths; it is curious, but it isn't pleasing. As the Indian Pipe could not be lured within garden walls, I will not write of it here, save to say that no one could ever see it growing in its shadowy home in the woods without yielding to its air of mystery. It is the weirdest flower that grows, so palpably ghastly that we feel almost a cheerful satisfaction in the perfection of its performance and our own responsive thrill, just as we do in a good ghost story.

—FROM *OLD TIME GARDENS*

THE ANEMONE

HARTLEY COLERIDGE

Who would have thought a thing so slight,
So frail a birth of warmth and light,
A thing as weak as fear or shame,
Bearing thy weakness in thy name,—
Who would have thought of finding thee,
Thou delicate Anemone,
Whose faintly tinted petals may
By any wind be torn away,
Whose many anthers with their dust,
And the dark purple dome their centre,
When winter strikes, soon as it likes,
Will quit their present rest, and must
Hurry away on wild adventure?
What power has given thee to outlast
The pelting rain, the driving blast;
To sit upon they slender stem,
A solitary diadem,
Adorning latest autumn with
A relic sweet of vernal pith?
Oh Heaven! if,—as faithful I believe,—
Thou wilt the prayer of faithful love receive,
Let it be so with me! I was a child
Of large belief, though froward, wild:
Gladly I listened to the holy word,
And deem'd my little prayers to God were heard.
All things I loved, however strange or odd,
As deeming all things were beloved by God.
In youth and manhood's careful sultry hours,
The garden of my youth bore many flowers
That now are faded; but my early faith,
Though thinner far than vapour, spectre, wraith,

Lighter than aught the rude wind blows away,
Has yet outlived the rude tempestuous day,
And may remain, a witness of the spring,
A sweet, a holy, and a lovely thing;
The promise of another spring to me,
My lovely, lone, and lost Anemone!

AMBLESIDE, NOVEMBER

KEN DRUSE

Japanese anemones
Bellevue, Washington

KEN DRUSE

Tobacco plants (*Nicotiana sylvestris*),
ornamental grasses, sedums, and
Boltonia asteroides
Boylston, Massachusetts

THE PASSING OF SUMMER

E. A. BOWLES

Some people prefer to read a sad note in Autumn and to dwell on the fading and passing of Summer's joys, and as it takes all sorts to make a world, and there must ever be those who *enjoy* bad health, who would miss their death's head as much as their salt-cellar on their dinner tables, we must allow them their minor harmonies and depressing remarks about departing swallows. But the good gardener should have no time to look back on departing joys; he should be all alive to take advantage of the yet warm soil, that, combined with a cool and moist atmosphere, makes the days of September and early October the most propitious of all the year for planting out recently collected alpines, nursed into vigour in shaded frames, or seedlings pricked out in boxes or beds, as well as for dividing and moving many of the plants of the garden; and yet again for that most fascinating part of gardening, the ordering and planting of the Season's bulbs.

—FROM *MY GARDEN IN AUTUMN AND WINTER*

HARRY
HARALAMBOU

leathers, heaths, and ornamental grass
Southold, New York

SEGOVIA — MADRID

LAURIE LEE

A few miles south of Segovia, at the foot of the sierras, I came on the royal gardens of La Granja—acres of writhing statues, walks, and fountains rising from the dust like a mirage. It was a grandiose folly, as large as Versailles and even more extravagant, and I found it in the peak of bloom and entirely deserted except for a few old gardeners with brooms.

A hundred fountains were playing, filling the sky with rainbows and creating an extraordinary dreamlike clamour. Marble gods and wood nymphs, dolphins and dragons, their anatomies studded with pipes and nozzles, directed complex cascades at one another or shot them high above the flowering trees. Everything that could be done with water seemed to be going on here, almost to the point of hydromania. Lakes, pools, jets and falls, flooded grottoes and exotic canals, all throbbed and surged at different levels, reflecting classical arbours, paths, and terraces, or running like cooling milk down the statuary.

Yet there was nobody to see it. Nobody but me—except, of course, for the gardeners, who went shuffling about as though under some timeless instruction, preparing for the return of some long-dead queen.

I stayed in the gardens for an hour or more, furtively paddling among the trickling leaves. The fountains, I learned later, played only on rare occasions, and I don't know why they played that day. It was like the winding-up of some monarch's toy, of which the owner had rapidly tired, and which now lay abandoned at the foot of the mountain together with its aged keepers. The fact was that La Granja, when looked at closely, was more than a little vulgar—a royal inflation of a suburban mind, a costly exercise with gnomes and toadstools.

—FROM *As I Walked Out One Midsummer Morning*

GARDENS
AND FIRELIGHT

HOMER

To left and right, outside, he saw an orchard
closed by a pale—four spacious acres planted
with trees in bloom or weighted down for picking:
pear trees, pomegranates, brilliant apples,
luscious figs, and olives ripe and dark.
Fruit never failed upon these trees: winter
and summer time they bore for through the year
the breathing Westwind ripened all in turn—
so one pear came to prime, and then another
and so with apples, figs and the vine's fruit
empurpled in the royal vineyard there.
Currants were dried at one end, on a platform
bare to the sun, beyond the vintage arbors
and vats the vintners trod; while near at hand
were new grapes barely formed as the green bloom fell,
or half-ripe clusters, faintly coloring.
After the vines came rows of vegetables
of all the kinds that flourish in every season,
and through the garden plots and orchard ran
channels from one clear fountain, while another
gushed through a pipe under the courtyard entrance
to serve the house and all who came for water.
These were the gifts of heaven to Alkínoös.

—FROM *THE ODYSSEY*

MICK HALES

Apple orchard at Tenbury Wells
Worcester, England

P I N G
A M R A N A N D

Garden at Sambō-in (Daigo-ji)
Kyoto, Japan

THE SAND GARDEN

ITALO CALVINO

A little courtyard covered with a white sand, thick-grained, almost gravel, raked in straight, parallel furrows or in concentric circles, around five irregular groups of stones or low boulders. This is one of the most famous monuments of Japanese civilization, the garden of rocks and sand of the Ryoanji of Kyoto, the image typical of that contemplation of the absolute to be achieved with the simplest means and without recourse to concepts capable of verbal expression, according to the teaching of the Zen monks, the most spiritual of Buddhist sects.

The rectangular enclosure of colorless sand is flanked on three sides by walls surmounted by tiles, beyond which is the green of trees. On the fourth side is a wooden platform, of steps, where the public can file by or linger and sit down. "Absorbed in this scene," explains the pamphlet offered to visitors, in Japanese and in English, signed by the abbot of the temple, "we, who think of ourselves as relative, are filled with serene wonder as we intuit Absolute Self, and our stained minds are purified."

Mr. Palomar is prepared to accept this advice on faith, and he sits on the steps, observes the rocks one by one, follows the undulations of the white sand, allows the undefinable harmony that links the elements of the picture gradually to pervade him.

Or, rather, he tries to imagine all these things as they would be felt by someone who could concentrate on looking at the Zen garden in solitude and silence. Because—we had forgotten to say—Mr. Palomar is crammed on the platform in the midst of hundreds of visitors, who jostle him on every side; camera lenses and movie cameras force their way past the elbows, knees, ears of the crowd, to frame the rocks and the sand from every angle, illuminated by natural light or by flashbulbs. Swarms of feet in wool socks step over him (shoes, as always in Japan, are left at the entrance); numerous offspring are thrust to the front row by pedagogical parents; clumps of uniformed students shove one another, eager only to conclude as quickly as possible this school outing to the famous monument; earnest visitors nodding their heads rhythmically check and make sure that everything written in the guidebook corresponds to reality and that everything seen in reality is also mentioned in the guide.

"We can view the garden as a group of mountainous islands in a great ocean, or as mountain tops rising above a sea of clouds. We can see it as a picture framed by the ancient mud walls, or we can forget the frame as we sense the truth of this sea stretching out boundlessly."

These "instructions for use" are contained in the leaflet, and to Mr. Palomar they seem perfectly plausible and immediately applicable,

HARRY
HARALAMBOU

Garden at Ryōan-ji
Kyoto, Japan

without effort, provided one is really sure of having a personality to shed, of looking at the world from inside an ego that can be dissolved, to become only a gaze. But it is precisely this outset that demands an effort of supplementary imagination, very difficult to muster when one's ego is glued into a solid crowd looking through its thousand eyes and walking on its thousand feet along the established itinerary of the tourist visit.

Must the conclusion be that the Zen mental techniques for achieving extreme humility, detachment from all possessiveness and pride, require as their necessary background aristocratic privilege, and assume an individualism with so much space and so much time around it, the horizons of a solitude free of anguish?

But this conclusion, which leads to the familiar lament over a paradise lost in the spread of mass civilization, sounds too facile for Mr. Palomar. He prefers to take a more difficult path, to try to grasp what the Zen garden can give him, looking at it in the only situation in which it can be looked at today, craning his neck among other necks.

What does he see? He sees the human race in the era of great numbers, which extends in a crowd, leveled but still made up of distinct individualities like the sea of grains of sand that submerges the surface of the world. . . . He sees that the world, nevertheless, continues to turn the boulder-backs of its nature indifferent to the fate of mankind, its hard substance that cannot be reduced to human assimilation. . . . He sees the forms in which the assembled human sand tends to arrange itself along lines of movement, patterns that combine regularity and fluidity like the rectilinear or circular tracks of a rake. . . . And between mankind-sand and world-boulder there is a sense of possible harmony, as if between two nonhomogeneous harmonies: that of the nonhuman in a balance of forces that seems not to correspond to any pattern, and that of human structures, which aspires to the rationality of a geometrical or musical composition, never definitive. . . .

—FROM MR. PALOMAR'S JOURNEYS

PLANTING BAMBOOS

PO CHÜ-I

Unrewarded, my will to serve the State;

At my closed door autumn grasses grow.

What could I do to ease a rustic heart?

I planted bamboos, more than a hundred shoots.

When I see their beauty, as they grow by the stream-side,

I feel again as though I lived in the hills,

And many a time on public holidays

Round their railing I walk till night comes.

Do not say that their roots are still weak,

Do not say that their shade is still small;

Already I feel that both in garden and house

Day by day a fresher air moves.

But most I love, lying near the window-side,

To hear in their branches the sound of the autumn-wind.

KEN DRUSE

Yellow-groove bamboos
(*Phyllostachys aureosulcata*) at
Blithewold Gardens and Arboretum
Bristol, Rhode Island

P I N G
A M R A N A N D

Chrysanthemums at Dumbarton Oaks
Washington, D.C.

THE CHRYSANTHEMUMS

JOHN STEINBECK

The high grey-flannel fog of winter closed off the Salinas Valley from the sky and from all the rest of the world. On every side it sat like a lid on the mountains and made of the great valley a closed pot. On the broad, level land floor the gang plows bit deep and left the black earth shining like metal where the shares had cut. On the foothill ranches across the Salinas River, the yellow stubble fields seemed to be bathed in cold sunshine, but there was no sunshine in the valley now in December. The thick willow scrub along the river flamed with sharp and positive yellow leaves.

It was a time of quiet and of waiting. The air was cold and tender. A light wind blew up from the southwest so that the farmers were mildly hopeful of a good rain before long; but fog and rain do not go together.

Across the river, on Henry Allen's foothill ranch there was little work to be done, for the hay was cut and stored and the orchards were plowed up to receive the rain deeply when it should come. The cattle on the higher slopes were becoming shaggy and rough-coated.

Elisa Allen, working in her flower garden, looked down across the yard and saw Henry, her husband, talking to two men in business suits. The three of them stood by the tractor shed, each man with one foot on the side of the little Fordson. They smoked cigarettes and studied the machine as they talked.

Elisa watched them for a moment and then went back to her work. She was thirty-five. Her face was lean and strong and her eyes were as clear as water. Her figure looked blocked and heavy in her gardening costume, a man's black hat pulled low down over her eyes, clodhopper shoes, a figured print dress almost completely covered by a big corduroy apron with four big pockets to hold the snips, the trowel and scratcher, the seeds and the knife she worked with. She wore heavy leather gloves to protect her hands while she worked.

She was cutting down the old year's chrysanthemum stalks with a pair of short and powerful scissors. She looked down toward the men by the tractor shed now and then. Her face was eager and mature and handsome; even her work with the scissors was over-eager, over-powerful. The chrysanthemum stems seemed too small and easy for her energy.

She brushed a cloud of hair out of her eyes with the back of her glove, and left a smudge of earth on her cheek in doing it. Behind her stood the neat white farm house with red geraniums close-banked around it as high as the windows. It was a hard-swept looking little house, with hard-polished windows, and a clean mud-mat on the front steps.

Elisa cast another glance toward the tractor shed. The strangers were getting into their Ford coupe. She took off a glove and put her strong fingers down into the forest of new green chrysanthemum sprouts that were growing around the old roots. She spread the leaves and looked down among the close-growing stems. No aphids were there, no sowbugs or snails or cutworms. Her terrier fingers destroyed such pests before they could get started.

Elisa started at the sound of her husband's voice. He had come near quietly, and he leaned over the wire fence that protected her flower garden from cattle and dogs and chickens.

"At it again," he said. "You've got a strong new crop coming."

Elisa straightened her back and pulled on the gardening glove again. "Yes. They'll be strong this coming year." In her tone and on her face there was a little smugness.

"You've got a gift with things," Henry observed. "Some of those yellow chrysanthemums you had this year were ten inches across. I wish you'd work out in the orchard and raise some apples that big."

Her eyes sharpened. "Maybe I could do it, too. I've a gift with things, all right. My mother had it. She could stick anything in the ground and make it grow. She said it was having planters' hands that knew how to do it."

"Well, it sure works with flowers," he said.

"Henry, who were those men you were talking to?"

"Why, sure, that's what I came to tell you. They were from the Western Meat Company. I sold those thirty head of three-year-old steers. Got nearly my own price, too."

"Good," she said. "Good for you."

"And I thought," he continued, "I thought how it's Saturday afternoon, and we might go into Salinas for dinner at a restaurant, and then to a picture show—to celebrate, you see."

"Good," she repeated. "Oh, yes. That will be good."

Henry put on his joking tone. "There's fights tonight. How'd you like to go to the fights?"

"Oh, no," she said breathlessly. "No, I wouldn't like fights."

"Just fooling, Elisa. We'll go to a movie. Let's see. It's two now. I'm going to take Scotty and bring down those steers from the hill. It'll take us maybe two hours. We'll go in town about five and have dinner at the Cominos Hotel. Like that?"

"Of course I'll like it. It's good to eat away from home."

"All right, then. I'll go get up a couple of horses."

She said, "I'll have plenty of time to transplant some of these sets, I guess."

She heard her husband calling Scotty down by the barn. And a little later she saw the two men ride up the pale yellow hillside in search of the steers.

There was a little square sandy bed kept for rooting the chrysanthemums. With her trowel she turned the soil over and over, and smoothed it and patted it firm. Then she dug ten parallel trenches to receive the sets. Back at the chrysanthemum bed she pulled out the little crisp shoots, trimmed off the leaves of each one with her scissors and laid it on a small orderly pile.

A squeak of wheels and plod of hoofs came from the road. Elisa looked up. The country road ran along the dense bank of willows and cottonwoods that bordered the river, and up this road came a curious vehicle, curiously drawn. It was an old spring-wagon, with a round canvas top on it like the cover of a prairie schooner. It was drawn by an old bay horse and a little grey-

and-white burro. A big stubble-bearded man sat between the cover flaps and drove the crawling team. Underneath the wagon, between the hind wheels, a lean and rangy mongrel dog walked sedately. Words were painted on the canvas, in clumsy, crooked letters. "Pots, pans, knives, sisors, lawn mores, Fixed." Two rows of articles, and the triumphantly definitive "Fixed" below. The black paint had run down in little sharp points beneath each letter.

Elisa, squatting on the ground, watched to see the crazy, loose-jointed wagon pass by. But it didn't pass. It turned into the farm road in front of her house, crooked old wheels skirling and squeaking. The rangy dog darted from between the wheels and ran ahead. Instantly the two ranch shepherds flew out at him. Then all three stopped, and with stiff and quivering tails, with taut straight legs, with ambassadorial dignity, they slowly circled, sniffing daintily. The caravan pulled up to Elisa's wire fence and stopped. Now the newcomer dog, feeling out-numbered, lowered his tail and retired under the wagon with raised hackles and bared teeth.

The man on the wagon seat called out, "That's a bad dog in a fight when he gets started."

Elisa laughed. "I see he is. How soon does he generally get started?"

The man caught up her laughter and echoed it heartily. "Sometimes not for weeks and weeks," he said. He climbed stiffly down, over the wheel. The horse and the donkey drooped like unwatered flowers.

Elisa saw that he was a very big man. Although his hair and beard were greying, he did not look old. His worn black suit was wrinkled and spotted with grease. The laughter had disappeared from his face and eyes the moment his laughing voice ceased. His eyes were dark, and they were full of the brooding that gets in the eyes of teamsters and of sailors. The calloused hands he rested on the wire fence were cracked, and every crack was a black line. He took off his battered hat.

"I'm off my general road, ma'am," he said. "Does this dirt road cut over across the river to the Los Angeles highway?"

Elisa stood up and shoved the thick scissors in her apron pocket. "Well, yes, it does, but it winds around and then fords the river. I don't think your team could pull through the sand."

He replied with some asperity, "It might surprise you what them beasts can pull through."

"When they get started?" she asked.

He smiled for a second. "Yes. When they get started."

"Well," said Elisa, "I think you'll save time if you go back to the Salinas road and pick up the highway there."

He drew a big finger down the chicken wire and made it sing. "I ain't in any hurry, ma'am. I go from Seattle to San Diego and back every year. Takes all my time. About six months each way. I aim to follow nice weather."

Elisa took off her gloves and stuffed them in the apron pocket with the scissors. She touched the under edge of her man's hat, searching for fugitive hairs. "That sounds like a nice kind of a way to live," she said.

He leaned confidentially over the fence. "Maybe you noticed the writing on my wagon. I mend pots and sharpen knives and scissors. You got any of them things to do?"

"Oh, no," she said quickly. "Nothing like that." Her eyes hardened with resistance.

"Scissors is the worst thing," he explained.

"Most people just ruin scissors trying to sharpen 'em, but I know how. I got a special tool. It's a little bobbit kind of thing, and patented. But it sure does the trick."

"No. My scissors are all sharp."

"All right, then. Take a pot," he continued earnestly, "a bent pot, or a pot with a hole. I can make it like new so you don't have to buy no new ones. That's a saving for you."

"No," she said shortly. "I tell you I have nothing like that for you to do."

His face fell to an exaggerated sadness. His voice took on a whining undertone. "I ain't had a thing to do today. Maybe I won't have no supper tonight. You see I'm off my regular road. I know folks on the highway clear from Seattle to San Diego. They save their things for me to sharpen up because they know I do it so good and save them money."

"I'm sorry," Elisa said irritably. "I haven't anything for you to do."

His eyes left her face and fell to searching the ground. They roamed about until they came to the chrysanthemum bed where she had been working. "What's them plants, ma'am?"

The irritation and resistance melted from Elisa's face. "Oh, those are chrysanthemums, giant whites and yellows. I raise them every year, bigger than anybody around here."

"Kind of a long-stemmed flower? Looks like a quick puff of colored smoke?" he asked.

"That's it. What a nice way to describe them."

"They smell kind of nasty till you get used to them," he said.

"It's a good bitter smell," she retorted, "not nasty at all."

He changed his tone quickly. "I like the smell myself."

"I had ten-inch blooms this year," she said.

The man leaned farther over the fence. "Look. I know a lady down the road a piece, has got the nicest garden you ever seen. Got nearly every kind of flower but no chrysantheums. Last time I was mending a copper-bottom washtub for her (that's a hard job but I do it good), she said to me, 'If you ever run acrost some nice chrysantheums I wish you'd try to get me a few seeds.' That's what she told me."

Elisa's eyes grew alert and eager. "She couldn't have known much about chrysanthemums. You can raise them from seed, but it's much easier to root the little sprouts you see there."

"Oh," he said. "I s'pose I can't take none to her, then."

"Why yes you can," Elisa cried. "I can put some in damp sand, and you can carry them right along with you. They'll take root in the pot if you keep them damp. And then she can transplant them."

"She'd sure like to have some, ma'am. You say they're nice ones?"

"Beautiful," she said. "Oh, beautiful." Her eyes shone. She tore off the battered hat and shook out her dark pretty hair. "I'll put them in a flower pot, and you can take them right with you. Come into the yard."

While the man came through the picket gate Elisa ran excitedly along the geranium-bordered path to the back of the house. And she returned carrying a big red flower pot. The gloves were forgotten now. She kneeled on the ground by the starting bed and dug up the sandy soil with her fingers and scooped it into the bright new flower pot. Then she picked up the little pile of shoots she had prepared. With her strong fingers she pressed them into the sand and tamped around them with her knuckles. The man stood over her. "I'll tell you what to do," she said. "You remember so you can tell the lady."

"Yes, I'll try to remember."

"Well, look. These will take root in about a month. Then she must set them out, about a foot apart in good rich earth like this, see?" She lifted a handful of dark soil for him to look at. "They'll grow fast and tall. Now remember this: In July tell her to cut them down, about eight inches from the ground."

"Before they bloom?" he asked.

"Yes, before they bloom." Her face was tight with eagerness. "They'll grow right up again. About the last of September the buds will start."

She stopped and seemed perplexed. "It's the budding that takes the most care," she said hesitantly. "I don't know how to tell you." She looked deep into his eyes, searchingly. Her mouth opened a little, and she seemed to be listening. "I'll try to tell you," she said. "Did you ever hear of planting hands?"

"Can't say I have, ma'am."

"Well, I can only tell you what it feels like. It's when you're picking off the buds you don't want. Everything goes right down into your fin-

Chrysanthemums and rhododendron
Media, Pennsylvania

gertips. You watch your fingers work. They do it themselves. You can feel how it is. They pick and pick the buds. They never make a mistake. They're with the plant. Do you see? Your fingers and the plant. You can feel that, right up your arm. They know. They never make a mistake. You can feel it. When you're like that you can't do anything wrong. Do you see that? Can you understand that?"

She was kneeling on the ground looking up at him. Her breast swelled passionately.

The man's eyes narrowed. He looked away self-consciously. "Maybe I know," he said. "Sometimes in the night in the wagon there—"

Elisa's voice grew husky. She broke in on him, "I've never lived as you do, but I know what you mean. When the night is dark—why, the stars are sharp-pointed, and there's quiet. Why, you rise up and up! Every pointed star gets driven into your body. It's like that. Hot and sharp and—lovely."

Kneeling there, her hand went out toward his legs in the greasy black trousers. Her hesitant fingers almost touched the cloth. Then her hand dropped to the ground. She crouched low like a fawning dog.

He said, "It's nice, just like you say. Only when you don't have no dinner, it ain't."

She stood up then, very straight, and her face was ashamed. She held the flower pot out to him and placed it gently in his arms. "Here. Put it in your wagon, on the seat, where you can watch it. Maybe I can find something for you to do."

At the back of the house she dug in the can pile and found two old and battered aluminum saucepans. She carried them back and gave them to him. "Here, maybe you can fix these."

His manner changed. He became profes-

sional. "Good as new I can fix them." At the back of his wagon he set a little anvil, and out of an oily tool box dug a small machine hammer. Elisa came through the gate to watch him while he pounded out the dents in the kettles. His mouth grew sure and knowing. At a difficult part of the work he sucked his under-lip.

"You sleep right in the wagon?" Elisa asked.

"Right in the wagon, ma'am. Rain or shine I'm dry as a cow in there."

"It must be nice," she said. "It must be very nice. I wish women could do such things."

"It ain't the right kind of a life for a woman."

Her upper lip raised a little, showing her teeth. "How do you know? How can you tell?" she said.

"I don't know, ma'am," he protested. "Of course I don't know. Now here's your kettles, done. You don't have to buy no new ones."

"How much?"

"Oh, fifty cents'll do. I keep my prices down and my work good. That's why I have all them satisfied customers up and down the highway."

Elisa brought him a fifty-cent piece from the house and dropped it in his hand. "You might be surprised to have a rival some time. I can sharpen scissors, too. And I can beat the dents out of little pots. I could show you what a woman might do."

He put his hammer back in the oily box and shoved the little anvil out of sight. "It would be a lonely life for a woman, ma'am, and a scarey life, too, with animals creeping under the wagon all night." He climbed over the single-tree, steadying himself with a hand on the burro's white rump. He settled himself in the seat, picked up the lines. "Thank you kindly, ma'am," he said. "I'll do like you told me; I'll go back and catch the Salinas road."

"Mind," she called, "if you're long in getting there, keep the sand damp."

"Sand, ma'am? . . . Sand? Oh, sure. You mean around the chrysantheums. Sure I will." He clucked his tongue. The beasts leaned luxuriously into their collars. The mongrel dog took his place between the back wheels. The wagon turned and crawled out the entrance road and back the way it had come, along the river.

Elisa stood in front of her wire fence watching the slow progress of the caravan. Her shoulders were straight, her head thrown back, her eyes half-closed, so that the scene came vaguely into them. Her lips moved silently, forming the words "Good-bye—good-bye." Then she whispered, "That's a bright direction. There's a glowing there." The sound of her whisper startled her. She shook herself free and looked about to see whether anyone had been listening. Only the dogs had heard. They lifted their heads toward her from their sleeping in the dust, and then stretched out their chins and settled asleep again. Elisa turned and ran hurriedly into the house.

In the kitchen she reached behind the stove and felt the water tank. It was full of hot water from the noonday cooking. In the bathroom she tore off her soiled clothes and flung them into the corner. And then she scrubbed herself with a little block of pumice, legs and thighs, loins and chest and arms, until her skin was scratched and red. When she had dried herself she stood in front of a mirror in her bedroom and looked at her body. She tightened her stomach and threw out her chest. She turned and looked over her shoulder at her back.

After a while she began to dress, slowly. She put on her newest underclothing and her nicest stockings and the dress which was the symbol of her prettiness. She worked carefully on her hair, penciled her eyebrows and rouged her lips.

Before she was finished she heard the little thunder of hoofs and the shouts of Henry and his helper as they drove the red steers into the corral. She heard the gate bang shut and set herself for Henry's arrival.

His step sounded on the porch. He entered the house calling, "Elisa, where are you?"

"In my room, dressing. I'm not ready. There's hot water for your bath. Hurry up. It's getting late."

When she heard him splashing in the tub, Elisa laid his dark suit on the bed, and shirt and socks and tie beside it. She stood his polished shoes on the floor beside the bed. Then she went to the porch and sat primly and stiffly down. She looked toward the river road where the willow-line was still yellow with frosted leaves so that under the high grey fog they seemed a thin band of sunshine. This was the only color in the grey afternoon. She sat unmoving for a long time. Her eyes blinked rarely.

Henry came banging out of the door, shoving his tie inside his vest as he came. Elisa stiffened and her face grew tight. Henry stopped short and looked at her. "Why—why, Elisa. You look so nice!"

"Nice? You think I look nice? What do you mean by 'nice'?"

Henry blundered on. "I don't know. I mean you look different, strong and happy."

"I am strong? Yes, strong. What do you mean 'strong'?"

He looked bewildered. "You're playing some kind of game," he said helplessly. "It's a kind of play. You look strong enough to break a calf over your knee, happy enough to eat it like a watermelon."

For a second she lost her rigidity. "Henry! Don't talk like that. You didn't know what you said." She grew complete again. "I'm strong," she boasted. "I never knew before how strong."

Henry looked down toward the tractor shed, and when he brought his eyes back to her, they were his own again. "I'll get out the car. You can put on your coat while I'm starting."

Elisa went into the house. She heard him drive to the gate and idle down his motor, and then she took a long time to put on her hat. She pulled it here and pressed it there. When Henry turned the motor off she slipped into her coat and went out.

The little roadster bounced along on the dirt road by the river, raising the birds and driving the rabbits into the brush. Two cranes flapped heavily over the willow-line and dropped into the river-bed.

Far ahead on the road Elisa saw a dark speck. She knew.

She tried not to look as they passed it, but her eyes would not obey. She whispered to herself sadly, "He might have thrown them off the road. That wouldn't have been much trouble, not very much. But he kept the pot," she explained. "He had to keep the pot. That's why he couldn't get them off the road."

The roadster turned a bend and she saw the caravan ahead. She swung full around toward her husband so she could not see the little covered wagon and the mismatched team as the car passed them.

In a moment it was over. The thing was done. She did not look back.

She said loudly, to be heard above the motor, "It will be good, tonight, a good dinner."

"Now you're changed again," Henry complained. He took one hand from the wheel and patted her knee. "I ought to take you in to dinner oftener. It would be good for both of us. We get so heavy out on the ranch."

"Henry," she asked, "could we have wine at dinner?"

"Sure we could. Say! That will be fine."

She was silent for a while; then she said, "Henry, at those prize fights, do the men hurt each other very much?"

"Sometimes a little, not often. Why?"

"Well, I've read how they break noses, and blood runs down their chests. I've read how the fighting gloves get heavy and soggy with blood."

He looked around at her. "What's the matter, Elisa? I didn't know you read things like that." He brought the car to a stop, then turned to the right over the Salinas River bridge.

"Do any women ever go to the fights?" she asked.

"Oh, sure, some. What's the matter, Elisa? Do you want to go? I don't think you'd like it, but I'll take you if you really want to go."

She relaxed limply in the seat. "Oh, no. No. I don't want to go. I'm sure I don't." Her face was turned away from him. "It will be enough if we can have wine. It will be plenty." She turned up her coat collar so he could not see that she was crying weakly—like an old woman.

IT MAY NOT COMFORT YOU

ROBERT FRANCIS

It may not comfort you to know—
But if the time should ever come
When lily and delphinium
Are trampled to their doom
And only weeds are left to grow—

(Where has the gardener gone?
And who will mow the lawn?)

It may be comfort in your need
To find the goldenrod in bloom,
To find it flower and not weed.

MICK HALES

Goldenrod
Southampton, New York

ITALIAN GARDEN-MAGIC

EDITH WHARTON

Though it is an exaggeration to say that there are no flowers in Italian gardens, yet to enjoy and appreciate the Italian garden-craft one must always bear in mind that it is independent of floriculture.

The Italian garden does not exist for its flowers; its flowers exist for it: they are a late and infrequent adjunct to its beauties, a parenthetical grace counting only as one more touch in the general effect of enchantment. This is no doubt partly explained by the difficulty of cultivating any but spring flowers in so hot and dry a climate, and the result has been a wonderful development of the more permanent effects to be obtained from the three other factors in garden-composition—marble, water and perennial verdure—and the achievement, by their skilful blending, of a charm independent of the seasons.

It is hard to explain to the modern garden-lover, whose whole conception of the charm of gardens is formed of successive pictures of flower-loveliness, how this effect of enchantment can be produced by anything so dull and monotonous as a mere combination of clipped green and stone-work.

The traveller returning from Italy, with his eyes and imagination full of the ineffable Italian garden-magic, knows vaguely that the enchantment exists; that he has been under its spell, and that it is more potent, more enduring, more intoxicating to every sense than the most elaborate and glowing effects of modern horticulture;

but he may not have found the key to the mystery. Is it because the sky is bluer, because the vegetation is more luxuriant? Our midsummer skies are almost as deep, our foliage is as rich, and perhaps more varied; there are, indeed, not a few resemblances between the North American summer climate and that of Italy in spring and autumn.

Some of those who have fallen under the spell are inclined to ascribe the Italian garden-magic to the effect of time; but, wonder-working as this undoubtedly is, it leaves many beauties unaccounted for. To seek the answer one must go deeper: the garden must be studied in relation to the house, and both in relation to the landscape. The garden of the Middle Ages, the garden one sees in old missal illuminations and in early woodcuts, was a mere patch of ground within the castle precincts, where "simples" were grown around a central well-head and fruit was espaliered against the walls. But in the rapid flowering of Italian civilization the castle walls were soon thrown down, and the garden expanded, taking in the fish-pond, the bowling-green, the rose-arbour and the clipped walk. The Italian country house, especially in the centre and the south of Italy, was almost always built on a hillside, and one day the architect looked forth from the terrace of his villa, and saw that, in his survey of the garden, the enclosing landscape was naturally included: the two formed a part of the same composition.

CURTICE
TAYLOR

Garden at Isola Bella
Lake Maggiore, Italy

The recognition of this fact was the first step in the development of the great garden-art of the Renaissance: the next was the architect's discovery of the means by which nature and art might be fused in his picture. He had now three problems to deal with: his garden must be adapted to the architectural lines of the house it adjoined; it must be adapted to the requirements of the inmates of the house, in the sense of providing shady walks, sunny bowling-greens, parterres and orchards, all conveniently accessible; and lastly it must be adapted to the landscape around it. At no time and in no country has this triple problem been so successfully dealt with as in the treatment of the Italian country house from the beginning of the sixteenth to the end of the eighteenth century; and in the blending of different elements, the subtle transition from the fixed and formal lines of art to the shifting and irregular lines of nature, and lastly in the essential convenience and livableness of the garden, lies the fundamental secret of the old garden-magic.

However much other factors may contribute to the total impression of charm, yet by eliminating them one after another, by *thinking away* the flowers, the sunlight, the rich tinting of time, one finds that, underlying all these, there is the deeper harmony of design which is independent of any adventitious effects. This does not imply that a plan of an Italian garden is as beautiful as the garden itself. The more permanent materials of which the latter is made— the stonework, the evergreen foliage, the effects of rushing or motionless water, above all the lines of the natural scenery—all form a part of the artist's design. But these things are as beautiful at one season as at another; and even these are but the accessories of the fundamental plan. The inherent beauty of the garden lies in the grouping of its parts—in the converging lines of its long ilex-walks, the alternation of sunny open spaces with cool woodland shade, the proportion between terrace and bowling-green, or between the height of a wall and the width of a path. None of these details was negligible to the landscape-architect of the Renaissance: he considered the distribution of shade and sunlight, of straight lines of masonry and rippled lines of foliage, as carefully as he weighed the relation of his whole composition to the scene about it.

—FROM *ITALIAN VILLAS AND THEIR GARDENS*

KEN DRUSE

Dahlias and annual pennisetum at
Blithewold Gardens and Arboretum
Bristol, Rhode Island

190

OLD-FASHIONED FLOWERS

MAURICE MAETERLINCK

Old flowers, I said. I was wrong; for they are not so old. When we study their history and investigate their pedigrees, we learn with surprise that most of them, down to the simplest and commonest, are new beings, freedmen, exiles, new-comers, visitors, foreigners. Any botanical treatise will reveal their origins. The Tulip, for instance (remember La Bruyère's "Solitary," "Oriental," "Agate," and "Cloth of Gold"), came from Constantinople in the sixteenth century. The Ranuncula, the Lunaria, the Maltese Cross, the Balsam, the Fuchsia, the African Marigold, or Tagetes Erecta, the Rose Campion, or Lychnis Coronaria, the two-coloured Aconite, the Amaranthus Caudatus, or Love-lies-bleeding, the Hollyhock and the Campanula Pyramidalis arrived at about the same time from the Indies, Mexico, Persia, Syria and Italy. The Pansy appears in 1613; the Yellow Alyssum in 1710; the Perennial Flax in 1775; the Scarlet Flax in 1819; the Purple Scabious in 1629; the Saxifraga Sarmentosa in 1771; the long-leaved Veronica in 1713; the Perennial Phlox is a little older. The Indian Pink made its entrance into our gardens about 1713.

The Garden Pink is of modern date. The Portulaca did not make her appearance till 1828; the Scarlet Sage till 1822. The Ageratum, or Coelestinum, now so plentiful and so popular, is not two centuries old. The Helichrysum, or Everlasting, is even younger. The Zinnia is exactly a centenarian. The Spanish Bean, a native of South America, and the Sweet Pea, an immigrant from Sicily, number a little over two hundred years. The Anthemis, whom we find in the least-known villages, has been cultivated only since 1699. The charming blue Lobelia of our borders came to us from the Cape of Good Hope at the time of the French Revolution. The China Aster, or Reine Marguerite, is dated 1731. The Annual or Drummond's Phlox, now so common, was sent over from Texas in 1835. The large-flowered Lavatera, who looks so confirmed a native, so simple a rustic, has blossomed in our gardens only since two centuries and a half; and the Petunia since some twenty lustres. The Mignonette, the Heliotrope—who would believe it?—are not two hundred years old. The Dahlia was born in 1802; and the Gladiolus is of yesterday.

—FROM *THE DOUBLE GARDEN*

BONSAI

LEONARD COCHRAN

Old man, precarious
on splayed feet,

leaning over the rim
of the known world,

gnarled, angled
(as we imagine age),

short of breadth,
he speaks of the past,

knowing in his roots
many tall stories.

CURTICE
TAYLOR

Bonsai at Longwood Gardens
Kennett Square, Pennsylvania

THE COUNTRY HOUSE-WIFE'S GARDEN

WILLIAM LAWSON

The number of formes, Mazes and Knots is so great, and men are so diversely delighted, that I leave every House-wife to her selfe, especially seeing to set downe many, had been but to fill much paper; yet lest I deprive her of all delight and direction, let her view these few, choyse, new formes, and note this generally, that all plots are square, and all are bordered about with Privit, Raisins, Fea-berries, Roses, Thorne, Rosemary, Bee-flowers, Isop, Sage, or such like.

W I N T E R

THOUGHTS THAT COME

ALFRED SIMSON

Sometimes I think the garden is even more beautiful in its winter garb than in its gala dress of summer. I know I have thought so more than once when every leaf and branch was clothed with a pure garment of snow, so light as not to hide the grace of form. But nothing, it seems to me, could ever transcend the exquisite beauty of the vegetation when on one occasion a sharp frost followed a very wet fog. The mist driven by the wind had imparted a coating of fresh moisture, evenly distributed, over and under every leaf and twig *inside* the trees and shrubs as well as outside. The light coating then froze and left every innermost twig resplendent with delicate white crystals. It was quite different from an ordinary frost or a fall of snow, beautiful as are frequently the effects of these. But the glory of the scene reached its climax when the sun came out and the thicket scintillated from the center as well as from its external surface.

Its dazzling splendor, however, could not last, and the glistening and enchanted spectacle gradually melted away before the greater and more glorious life-giving presence of "God's lidless Eye." This gorgeous scene, however, has always dwelt in my memory, and figures as the most glowing aspect a garden can assume at any season of the year.

—FROM *GARDEN MOSAICS*

H U G H
P A L M E R

Hydrangea macrophylla at
Brook Cottage
Oxfordshire, England

HUGH
PALMER

Persian ivy (*Hedera colchica*
'Dentato-variegata') at Epwell Mill
Oxfordshire, England

197

SUN-DIAL INSCRIPTION

TIME'S GLASS AND SCYTHE
THY LIFE AND DEATH DECLARE.
SPEND WELL THY TIME
AND FOR DEATH PREPARE.

MICK HALES

Rose garden
Philadelphia, Pennsylvania

199

MICK HALES

Apple trees
La Malbaie, Canada

THE GARDENER'S DECEMBER

KAREL ČAPEK

Yes, you are right, everything is now finished. Until now he has hoed, dug, loosened, turned over, manured, and dressed with lime; strewn the soil over with peat, ashes, soot; cut, sown, planted, transplanted, divided, put bulbs in the ground, and taken out tubers for the winter; sprinkled and watered, cut the grass, weeded, covered the plants with brushwood, or raked soil to their necks—all this he did between February and December, and only now, when the garden is buried in snow, does he remember that he has forgotten something: to look at it. For you must know that until now he has had no time to do that. When in summer he ran to look at a flowering gentian he had to stop on the way to weed the grass. When he wanted to enjoy the beauty of delphiniums in bloom he found that he had to give them supports. When asters came into flower he ran to fetch a can to water them. When phlox flowered he pulled out couch-grass; when roses were in bloom he looked where to cut side-branches, or how to destroy rust; when chrysanthemums began to open he

ran for a hoe to loosen the soil which had settled round their roots. What you do expect? There was always something to do; how, then, could be put his hands in his pockets and just look to see what things are like?

Now, thank God, everything is finished; perhaps there are still things to be done; there at the back the soil is like lead, and I rather wanted to transplant this centaurea, but peace be with you; the snow has already fallen. What would you say, gardener, if for the first time you *looked at* your garden?

Well, this black thing here, which is sticking out of the snow, is a withered viscaria; this dry stalk is a blue aquilegia; that tuft of shrivelled leaves is astilbe; and look, that sweep there is Aster ericoides; and here, where there is nothing at all, there is an orange trollius; and this heap of snow here is dianthus, of course it is dianthus. And that stem is perhaps the red yarrow.

Brr, it is cold! Even in winter one can't enjoy one's garden.

—FROM *THE GARDENER'S YEAR*

SONNET 5

WILLIAM SHAKESPEARE

Those hours, that with gentle work did frame
The lovely gaze where every eye doth dwell,
Will play the tyrants to the very same
And that unfair which fairly doth excel;
For never-resting time leads summer on
To hideous winter, and confounds him there;
Sap check'd with frost, and lusty leaves quite gone,
Beauty o'ersnow'd and bareness everywhere:
Then, were not summer's distillation left,
A liquid prisoner pent in walls of glass,
Beauty's effect with beauty were bereft,
Nor it, nor no remembrance what it was:

> But flowers distill'd, though they with winter meet,
> Leese but their show; their substance still lives sweet.

HUGH
PALMER

Chess set of clipped yew at
Hasely Court
Oxfordshire, England

I greatly admire Burle Marx for his originality and for the ferment he has started in the world of landscape architecture. I admire him, too, because he is a horticulturist and plant explorer, a gardener and botanist, as well as a designer of gardens and landscapes. He has sought out in the tropical forests of his continent trees of unusual form, studied their habits, and transplanted them to where they will thrive and become plastic forms that tie in with the buildings of Niemeyer and other modern architects. And Marx's small, intimate gardens can be just that—lush, private tropical retreats, with lotus in pools, or small made ponds crossed by stepping stones in the Japanese manner, surrounded by a fascinating variety of tropical trees and plants. No carpeting here, no intrusion on the genius of the place.

—FROM *ONWARD AND UPWARD IN THE GARDEN*

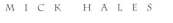

MICK HALES

Garden of Roberto Burle Marx
Near Rio de Janiero, Brazil

Palm garden
Near Rio de Janiero, Brazil

DICIONÁRIO

CLARICE LISPECTOR

PALM

The palm has no aroma. He gives of himself proudly (for he is a proud plant) in both shape and color. This plant is clearly male.

ORCHID

This flower is exquisite, a real beauty, and obnoxious. She lacks spontaneity; she requires a vase. But she is a splendid woman, there's no doubt about it. No denying, either, that she possesses nobility. The orchid is an epiphyte, that is, a flower which lives on the surface of another plant without deriving nutrition from it.

What I've said isn't true: I adore orchids.

PING AMRANAND

Hybrid orchid (× *Sophrolaeliocattleya*)
Kensington, Maryland

This is definitely a male flower. There is a dose of aggression in the way he loves, and in his healthy self-esteem. He has what appears to be a cockscomb, and he crows like a rooster except he doesn't wait for sunrise. When the sun is plainly in sight, this flower gives a cry of visual greeting to the world, since the world is always newly born.

PING
AMRANAND

False bird-of-paradise
(*Heliconia rostrata*)
Bali, Indonesia

PING
AMRANAND

Giant water lilies (*Victoria regia*)
Bangkok, Thailand

ROYAL WATER LILY

There are enormous ones, over six feet in diameter, in the Botanical Garden of Rio de Janeiro. They are aquatic and stunning to look at. They are greater Brazil. Royal water lilies are changeful: white on the first day, later pink and even reddish. They inspire peace and tranquility. Water lilies are at the same time simple and majestic. Although they float on the surface of the water, they give shade.

—FROM *A DESCOBERTA DO MUNDO*

209

KEN DRUSE

Moth orchids (*Phalaenopsis*) at the
New York Botanical Garden
Bronx, New York

THE FLOWERING OF THE STRANGE ORCHID

H. G. WELLS

The buying of orchids always has in it a certain speculative flavour. You have before you the brown shrivelled lump of tissue, and for the rest you must trust your judgment, or the auctioneer, or your good-luck, as your taste may incline. The plant may be moribund or dead, or it may be just a respectable purchase, fair value for your money, or perhaps—for the thing has happened again and again—there slowly unfolds before the delighted eyes of the happy purchaser, day after day, some new variety, some novel richness, a strange twist of the labellum, or some subtler colouration or unexpected mimicry. Pride, beauty, and profit blossom together on one delicate green spike, and, it may be, even immortality. For the new miracle of Nature may stand in need of a new specific name, and what so convenient as that of its discoverer? "Johnsmithia"! There have been worse names.

It was perhaps the hope of some such happy discovery that made Winter-Wedderburn such a frequent attendant at these sales—that hope, and also, maybe, the fact that he had nothing else of the slightest interest to do in the world. He was a shy, lonely, rather ineffectual man, provided with just enough income to keep off the spur of necessity, and not enough nervous energy to make him seek any exacting employment. He might have collected stamps or coins, or translated Horace, or bound books, or invented new species of diatoms. But, as it happened, he grew orchids, and had one ambitious little hothouse.

"I have a fancy," he said over his coffee, "that something is going to happen to me to-day." He spoke—as he moved and thought—slowly.

"Oh, don't say *that!*" said his housekeeper—who was also his remote cousin. For "something happening" was a euphemism that meant only one thing to her.

"You misunderstand me. I mean nothing unpleasant . . . though what I do mean I scarcely know.

"To-day," he continued, after a pause, "Peters' are going to sell a batch of plants from the Andamans and the Indies. I shall go up and see what they have. It may be I shall buy something good, unawares. That may be it."

He passed his cup for his second cupful of coffee.

"Are those the things collected by that poor young fellow you told me of the other day?" asked his cousin as she filled his cup.

"Yes," he said, and became meditative over a piece of toast.

"Nothing ever does happen to me," he remarked presently, beginning to think aloud. "I wonder why? Things enough happen to other people. There is Harvey. Only the other week—on Monday he picked up sixpence, on Wednesday his chicks all had the staggers, on Friday his cousin came home from Australia, and on Saturday he broke his ankle. What a whirl of excitement!—compared to me."

"I think I would rather be without so much excitement," said his housekeeper. "It can't be good for you."

"I suppose it's troublesome. Still . . . you see, nothing ever happens to me. When I was a little boy I never had accidents. I never fell in love as I grew up. Never married. . . . I wonder how it feels to have something happen to you, something really remarkable.

"That orchid-collector was only thirty-six—twenty years younger than myself—when he died. And he had been married twice and divorced once; he had had malarial fever four times, and once he broke his thigh. He killed a Malay once, and once he was wounded by a poisoned dart. And in the end he was killed by jungle-leeches. It must have all been very troublesome, but then it must have been very interesting, you know—except, perhaps, the leeches."

"I am sure it was not good for him," said the lady, with conviction.

"Perhaps not." And then Wedderburn looked at his watch. "Twenty-three minutes past eight. I am going up by the quarter to twelve train, so that there is plenty of time. I think I shall wear my alpaca jacket—it is quite warm enough—and my grey felt hat and brown shoes. I suppose——"

He glanced out of the window at the serene sky and sunlit garden, and then nervously at his cousin's face.

"I think you had better take an umbrella if you are going to London," she said in a voice that admitted of no denial. "There's all between here and the station coming back."

When he returned he was in a state of mild excitement. He had made a purchase. It was rare that he could make up his mind quickly enough to buy, but this time he had done so.

"There are Vandas," he said, "and a Dendrobe and some Palaeonophis." He surveyed his purchases lovingly as he consumed his soup. They were laid out on the spotless tablecloth before him, and he was telling his cousin all about them as he slowly meandered through his dinner. It was his custom to live all his visits to London over again in the evening for her and his own entertainment.

"I knew something would happen to-day. And I have bought all these. Some of them—some of them—I feel sure, do you know, that some of them will be remarkable. I don't know how it is, but I feel just as sure as if someone had told me that some of these will turn out remarkable.

"That one"—he pointed to a shrivelled rhizome—"was not identified. It may be a Palaeonophis—or it may not. It may be a new species, or even a new genus. And it was the last that poor Batten ever collected."

"I don't like the look of it," said his housekeeper. "It's such an ugly shape."

"To me it scarcely seems to have a shape."

"I don't like those things that stick out," said his housekeeper.

"It shall be put away in a pot to-morrow."

"It looks," said the housekeeper, "like a spider shamming dead."

Wedderburn smiled and surveyed the root with his head on one side. "It is certainly not a pretty lump of stuff. But you can never judge of these things from their dry appearance. It may turn out to be a very beautiful orchid indeed. How busy I shall be to-morrow! I must see to-night just exactly what to do with these things, and to-morrow I shall set to work.

"They found poor Batten lying dead, or dying, in a mangrove swamp—I forget which," he began again presently, "with one of these very orchids crushed up under his body. He had been unwell for some days with some kind of native fever, and I suppose he fainted. These mangrove swamps are very unwholesome. Every drop of blood, they say, was taken out of him by the jungle-leeches. It may be that very plant that cost him his life to obtain."

"I think none the better of it for that."

"Men must work though women may weep," said Wedderburn with profound gravity.

"Fancy dying away from every comfort in a nasty swamp! Fancy being ill of fever with nothing to take but chlorodyne and quinine—if men were left to themselves they would live on chlorodyne and quinine—and no one round you but horrible natives! They say the Andaman islanders are most disgusting wretches—and, anyhow, they can scarcely make good nurses, not having the necessary training. And just for people in England to have orchids!"

"I don't suppose it was comfortable, but some men seem to enjoy that kind of thing," said Wedderburn. "Anyhow, the natives of his party were sufficiently civilised to take care of all his collection until his colleague, who was an ornithologist, came back again from the interior; though they could not tell the species of the orchid and had let it wither. And it makes these things more interesting."

"It makes them disgusting. I should be afraid of some of the malaria clinging to them. And just think, there has been a dead body lying across that ugly thing! I never thought of that before. There! I declare I cannot eat another mouthful of dinner."

"I will take them off the table if you like, and put them in the window-seat. I can see them just as well there."

The next few days he was indeed singularly busy in his steamy little hothouse, fussing about with charcoal, lumps of teak, moss, and all the other mysteries of the orchid cultivator. He considered he was having a wonderfully eventful time. In the evening he would talk about these new orchids to his friends, and over and over again he reverted to his expectation of something strange.

Several of the Vandas and the Dendrobium died under his care, but presently the strange orchid began to show signs of life. He was delighted and took his housekeeper right away from jam-making to see it at once, directly he made the discovery.

"That is a bud," he said, "and presently there will be a lot of leaves there, and those little things coming out here are aërial rootlets."

"They look to me like little white fingers poking out of the brown," said his housekeeper. "I don't like them."

"Why not?"

"I don't know. They look like fingers trying to get at you. I can't help my likes and dislikes."

"I don't know for certain, but I don't *think* there are any orchids I know that have aërial rootlets quite like that. It may be my fancy, of course. You see they are a little flattened at the ends."

"I don't like 'em," said his housekeeper, suddenly shivering and turning away. "I know it's very silly of me—and I'm very sorry, particularly as you like the thing so much. But I can't help thinking of that corpse."

"But it may not be that particular plant. That was merely a guess of mine."

His housekeeper shrugged her shoulders. "Anyhow I don't like it," she said.

Wedderburn felt a little hurt at her dislike to the plant. But that did not prevent his talking to her about orchids generally, and this orchid in particular, whenever he felt inclined.

"There are such queer things about orchids," he said one day; "such possibilities of surprises. You know, Darwin studied their fertilisation, and showed that the whole structure of an ordinary orchid-flower was contrived in order that moths might carry the pollen from plant to plant. Well, it seems that there are lots of orchids known the flower of which cannot possibly be used for fertilisation in that way. Some of the Cypripediums, for instance; there are no insects known that can possibly fertilise them, and some of them have never been found with seed."

"But how do they form new plants?"

"By runners and tubers, and that kind of outgrowth. That is easily explained. The puzzle is, what are the flowers for?"

"Very likely," he added, "*my* orchid may be something extraordinary in that way. If so I shall study it. I have often thought of making researches as Darwin did. But hitherto I have not found the time, or something else has happened to prevent it. The leaves are beginning to unfold now. I do wish you would come and see them!"

But she said that the orchid-house was so hot it gave her the headache. She had seen the plant once again, and the aërial rootlets, which were now some of them more than a foot long, had unfortunately reminded her of tentacles reaching out after something; and they got into her dreams, growing after her with incredible rapidity. So that she had settled to her entire satisfaction that she would not see that plant again, and Wedderburn had to admire its leaves alone. They were of the ordinary broad form, and a deep glossy green, with splashes and dots of deep red towards the base. He knew of no other leaves quite like them. The plant was placed on a low bench near the thermometer, and close by was a simple arrangement by which a tap dripped on the hot-water pipes and kept the air steamy. And he spent his afternoons now with some regularity meditating on the approaching flowering of this strange plant.

And at last the great thing happened. Directly he entered the little glass house he knew that the spike had burst out, although his great *Palaeonophis Lowii* hid the corner where his new darling stood. There was a new odour in the air, a rich, intensely sweet scent, that overpowered every other in that crowded, steaming little greenhouse.

Directly he noticed this he hurried down to the strange orchid. And, behold! the trailing green spikes bore now three great splashes of blossom, from which this overpowering sweetness proceeded. He stopped before them in an ecstasy of admiration.

The flowers were white, with streaks of golden orange upon the petals; the heavy labellum was coiled into an intricate projection, and a wonderful bluish purple mingled there with the gold. He could see at once that the genus

Corsage orchids (*Cattleya*) at the
New York Botanical Garden
Bronx, New York

was altogether a new one. And the insufferable scent! How hot the place was! The blossoms swam before his eyes.

He would see if the temperature was right. He made a step towards the thermometer. Suddenly everything appeared unsteady. The bricks on the floor were dancing up and down. Then the white blossoms, the green leaves behind them, the whole greenhouse, seemed to sweep sideways, and then in a curve upward.

At half-past four his cousin made the tea, according to their invariable custom. But Wedderburn did not come in for his tea.

"He is worshipping that horrid orchid," she told herself, and waited ten minutes. "His watch must have stopped. I will go and call him."

She went straight to the hothouse, and, opening the door, called his name. There was no reply. She noticed that the air was very close, and loaded with an intense perfume. Then she saw something lying on the bricks between the hot-water pipes.

For a minute, perhaps, she stood motionless. He was lying, face upward, at the foot of the strange orchid. The tentacle-like aërial rootlets no longer swayed freely in the air, but were crowded together, a tangle of grey ropes, and stretched tight with their ends closely applied to his chin and neck and hands.

She did not understand. Then she saw from under one of the exultant tentacles upon his cheek there trickled a little thread of blood.

With an inarticulate cry she ran towards

Moth orchids (*Phalaenopsis*) at the
New York Botanical Garden
Bronx, New York

him, and tried to pull him away from the leech-like suckers. She snapped two of these tentacles, and their sap dripped red.

Then the overpowering scent of the blossom began to make her head reel. How they clung to him! She tore at the tough ropes, and he and the white inflorescence swam about her. She felt she was fainting, knew she must not. She left him and hastily opened the nearest door, and, after she had panted for a moment in the fresh air, she had a brilliant inspiration. She caught up a flower-pot and smashed in the windows at the end of the greenhouse. Then she reëntered. She tugged now with renewed strength at Wedderburn's motionless body, and brought the strange orchid crashing to the floor. It still clung with the grimmest tenacity to its victim. In a frenzy, she lugged it and him into the open air.

Then she thought of tearing through the sucker rootlets one by one, and in another minute she had released him and was dragging him away from the horror.

He was white and bleeding from a dozen circular patches.

The odd-job man was coming up the garden, amazed at the smashing of glass, and saw her emerge, hauling the inanimate body with red-stained hands. For a moment he thought impossible things.

"Bring some water!" she cried, and her voice dispelled his fancies. When, with unnatural alacrity, he returned with the water, he found her weeping with excitement, and with Wedderburn's head upon her knee, wiping the blood from his face.

"What's the matter?" said Wedderburn, opening his eyes feebly, and closing them again at once.

"Go and tell Annie to come out here to me, and then go for Doctor Haddon at once," she said to the odd-job man so soon as he brought the water; and added, seeing he hesitated, "I will tell you all about it when you come back."

Presently Wedderburn opened his eyes again, and, seeing that he was troubled by the puzzle of his position, she explained to him, "You fainted in the hothouse."

"And the orchid?"

"I will see to that," she said.

Wedderburn had lost a good deal of blood, but beyond that he had suffered no very great injury. They gave him brandy mixed with some pink extract of meat, and carried him upstairs to bed. His housekeeper told her incredible story in fragments to Dr. Haddon. "Come to the orchid-house and see," she said.

The cold outer air was blowing in through the open door, and the sickly perfume was almost dispelled. Most of the torn aërial rootlets lay already withered amidst a number of dark stains upon the bricks. The stem of the inflorescence was broken by the fall of the plant, and the flowers were growing limp and brown at the edges of the petals. The doctor stooped towards it, then saw that one of the aërial rootlets still stirred feebly, and hesitated.

The next morning the strange orchid still lay there, black now and putrescent. The door banged intermittently in the morning breeze, and all the array of Wedderburn's orchids was shrivelled and prostrate. But Wedderburn himself was bright and garrulous upstairs in the glory of his strange adventure.

THE TASK

WILLIAM COWPER

Who loves a garden loves a green-house too.
Unconscious of a less propitious clime,
There blooms exotic beauty, warm and snug,
While the winds whistle and the snows descend.
The spiry myrtle with unwith'ring leaf
Shines there, and flourishes. The golden boast
Of Portugal and western India there,
The ruddier orange, and the paler lime,
Peep through their polish'd foliage at the storm,
And seem to smile at what they need not fear.
Th' amomum there with intermingling flow'rs
And cherries hangs her twigs. Geranium boasts
Her crimson honours, and the spangled beau,
Ficoides, glitters bright the winter long.
All plants, of ev'ry leaf, that can endure
The winter's frown, if screen'd from his shrewd bite,
Live there, and prosper....

—FROM "THE TASK"

PING
AMRANAND

Regal geraniums (*Pelargonium* ×
domesticum) in a greenhouse
at Brynhyfryd
Corris, Wales

HUGH
PALMER

Original millrace at Epwell Mill
Oxfordshire, England

JANUARY IN SUSSEX WOODS

RICHARD JEFFERIES

The lost leaves measure our years; they are gone as the days are gone, and the bare branches silently speak of a new year, slowly advancing to its buds, its foliage, and fruit. Deciduous trees associate with human life as this yew never can. Clothed in its yellowish-green needles, its tarnished green, it knows no hope nor sorrow; it is indifferent to winter, and does not look forward to summer. With their annual loss of leaves, and renewal, oak and elm and ash and beech seem to stand by us and to share our thoughts. There is no wind at the edge of the wood, and the few flakes of snow that fall from the overcast sky flutter as they drop, now one side higher and then the other, as the leaves did in the still hours of autumn. The delicacy of the outer boughs of the great trees visible against the dark background of cloud is as beautiful in its own way as the massed foliage of summer. Each slender bough is drawn out to a line; line follows line as shade grows under the pencil, but each of these lines is separate. Great boles of beech, heavy timber at the foot, thus end at their summits in the lightest and most elegant pencilling. Where the birches are tall, sometimes the number and closeness of these bare sprays causes a thickening almost as if there were leaves there. The leaves, in fact, when they come, conceal the finish of the trees; they give colour, but they hide the beautiful structure under them.

—FROM *THE LIFE OF THE FIELDS*

FEBRUARY

JOSEPH WOOD KRUTCH

The most serious charge which can be brought against New England is not Puritanism but February. It is true that before we are finished with it the days are unmistakably longer than they were in December or January, and true that there are periods when the daylight is brighter, as well as longer. But these brief interludes are too infrequent to be counted on, and the relapses are so complete that the interludes do not seem even promises. Now more than ever one must remind oneself that it is wasteful folly to wish that time would pass, or—as the puritanical old saying used to have it—to kill time until time kills you. Spring is too far away to comfort even by anticipation, and winter long ago lost the charm of novelty. This is the very three A.M. of the calendar.

I will not say that I would like to dispense with February, for I should not willingly agree to make my life one-twelfth shorter—not even, I suppose, if it were going to be February all the year round. Nevertheless there are regions of the earth where the months bear the same names as ours but where the allotment of time to the various seasons has been more sensibly managed. Some of them, for instance, have a real November (in December), and a real December (in January), and then get on immediately to an April. That seems to me about right, and I would gladly exchange our February for another May; or, if that is asking too much, for another October; or for, indeed, almost anything else I was offered. There are some optimists who search eagerly for the skunk cabbage which in February sometimes pushes itself up through the ice, and who call it a sign of spring. I wish that I could feel that way about it, but I do not. The truth of the matter, to me, is simply that skunk cabbage blooms in the winter time. There is no more cold-blooded animal than your frog, and you will not catch him stirring now.

—FROM *THE TWELVE SEASONS*

KEN DRUSE

Skunk cabbage (*Symplocarpus
foetidus*) at the New Jersey State
Botanical Gardens at Skylands
Ringwood, New Jersey

223

HELLEBORE

COLETTE

Where we live, and to a lesser extent everywhere else, it is called the Christmas rose. Yet it does not resemble a rose, not even the little eglantine, nervous and blushing, except that it does have five petals like all the others.

A pebble, a blade of grass, a fallen leaf, all have more of a smell than it does. To be fragrant is not its mission. But let December come, let the wintry frost blanket us, and the hellebore will show you its true colors. A nice deep snow, not too powdery, a little heavy, and winter nights that the west wind passes through like a precursor, now that's what makes the hellebore happy. To the garden of my childhood, it was at the end of December that I would go, certain to find it there, and lift the slabs of snow that covered the winter rose.

Promised, unexpected, precious, and prostrate but fully alive, the hellebores hibernate. As long as they are weighed down with snow, they remain closed, ovoid, and on the outside of each furled convex petal a vaguely pink streak seems to be the only indication that they are breathing. The hardly, star-shaped leaves, the firmness of the stems, so many characteristics through which the whole plant proclaims its touching, evergreen determination. When picked, its sensitive little shells undo their seams in the warmth of a room, unleashing the little tuft of yellow stamens, happy to be alive and spreading, free . . . Hellebore! When you are put into the hands of the florist, his first concern is to manhandle your petals, bending them back flat, just as he attempts to do to the tulip, torturing it to death. Behind his back, I undo his work of breaking and entering, and if I can promise you, in my house, water up to the neck and light up to the eyelashes, you can sleep out the remainder of your chaste slumber, then perish by the decision of human hands, when the warm snow might still have kept you alive, hellebore.

—FROM *FLOWERS AND FRUIT*

MICK HALES

Helleborus sp. at the Cloisters
New York, New York

225

H U G H
P A L M E R

Snowdrops and Lenten roses
(*Helleborus orientalis*) at
Stone Cottage
Rutland, England

TO A SNOW-DROP, APPEARING VERY EARLY IN THE SEASON

WILLIAM WORDSWORTH

Lone Flower, hemmed in with snows and white as they
But hardier far, though modestly thou bend
Thy front—as if *such* presence could offend!
Who guards thy slender stalk while, day by day,
Storms, sallying from the mountain-tops, way-lay
The rising sun, and on the plains descend?
Accept the greeting that befits a friend
Whose zeal outruns his promise! Blue-eyed May
Shall soon behold this border thickly set
With bright jonquils, their odours lavishing
On the soft west-wind and his frolic peers;
Yet will I not thy gentle grace forget
Chaste Snow-drop, vent'rous harbinger of Spring,
And pensive monitor of fleeting years!

THE OTHER SIDE OF THE PICTURE

BEVERLEY NICHOLS

For many weeks I visited that patch of sloping ground where the Chionodoxa lay dormant. My diary is full of impatient entries about it. Thus:

NOVEMBER 30TH. No sign of Chionodoxa. Feel very depressed. Doubt if shall ever succeed in anything.

DECEMBER 15TH. No sign of Chionodoxa. Why do I live in this damned country? Had a letter from Willie Maugham today. They are bathing at Antibes.

JANUARY 18TH. No sign of Chionodoxa. If the government goes on spending money at this rate, there will be a flight from the pound.

FEBRUARY 3RD. No sign of Chionodoxa. My hair is coming out. Went yesterday to hair man. Says must have treatment. Will cost twelve guineas.

MARCH 3RD. No sign of Chionodoxa. Perhaps I should feel better if I had a real religion. But how *can* one have a real religion if one *wants* to have one so much? I mean, does not the *desire* in itself nullify the authenticity of the creed . . . which means nothing . . . but I am so terribly tired that I cannot phrase things properly.

MARCH 10TH. Signs of Chionodoxa! Really, at last, three wart-like objects have appeared. They are so late that one ought to have hit them on the head and told them to go back and come again next year. But one doesn't. Is one weak?

MARCH 20TH. *Two Chionodoxa out!* Ah, but it was worth waiting for! The most beautiful blue. Like the blue of a church window on a cold spring morning when the sun is behind it, and the starlings are shrill outside the porch. But I must not go on like this.

—FROM *DOWN THE GARDEN PATH*

PING
AMRANAND

Glory-of-the-snow (*Chionodoxas* sp.)
at Beech Terrace in Dumbarton Oaks
Washington, D.C.

BIOGRAPHIES

AUTHORS

MATTHEW ARNOLD (1822–1888) English poet and critic

BROOKS ATKINSON (b. 1894) American drama critic

W. H. AUDEN (1907–1973) English poet

WILLIAM BLAKE (1757–1827) English artist, poet, and mystic

E. A. BOWLES (1864–1954) English garden writer

ROBERT BRIDGES (1844–1930) English poet

FRANCES HODGSON BURNETT (1849–1924) English writer

ITALO CALVINO (b. 1923) Italian novelist and short-story writer

KAREL ČAPEK (1890–1938) Czech journalist, playwright, and novelist

LEWIS CARROLL (1832–1898) English writer, mathematician, and photographer

GEOFFREY CHAUCER (1340?–1400) English poet

(FR.) LEONARD COCHRAN, O. P. (b. 1928) American priest and poet

HARTLEY COLERIDGE (1796–1849) English writer

COLETTE (1873–1954) French novelist, essayist, playwright, and short-story writer

WILLIAM COWPER (1731–1800) English poet

EMILY DICKINSON (1830–1886) American poet

SIR KENELM DIGBY (1603–1665) English science and religion author

JOHN DONNE (1573–1631) English poet

ALICE MORSE EARLE (1853–1911) American writer

HENRY N. ELLACOMBE (1822–1916) British garden writer

HELEN MORGANTHAU FOX (1884–1974) American garden writer

ROBERT FRANCIS (1901–1987) American poet

ROBERT FROST (1874–1963) American poet

LEWIS GANNETT (1891–1966) American critic and author

FEDERICO GARCÍA LORCA (1898–1936) Spanish poet and playwright

DAVID GRAYSON (1870–1946) American journalist and author

MRS. EDWARD HARDING (d. 1938) American horticulturist and garden writer

NATHANIEL HAWTHORNE (1804–1864) American novelist and short-story writer

LAFCADIO HEARN (1850–1904) Greek-born American/Japanese writer

ROBERT HERRICK (1591–1674) English lyric poet

HOMER (900–800? B.C.) Ancient Greek epic poet

GERARD MANLEY HOPKINS (1844–1889) English Jesuit and poet

WASHINGTON IRVING (1783–1859) American satirist, short-story writer, and diplomat

RICHARD JEFFERIES (1848–1887) English naturalist and writer

JOSEPH WOOD KRUTCH (1893–1970) American critic and essayist

STANLEY KUNITZ (b. 1905) American poet, literary critic, and essayist

ELIZABETH LAWRENCE (1904–1985) American garden writer

WILLIAM LAWSON (b. 1904) English reverend and writer

LAURIE LEE (b. 1914) British playwright and poet

SUZANNAH LESSARD (b. 1944) American writer

DENISE LEVERTOV (b. 1923) American poet and essayist

CLARICE LISPECTOR (1925–1973) Brazilian novelist and short-story writer

AMY LOWELL (1874–1925) American poet and critic

ANTONIO MACHADO (1875–1939) Spanish poet

LOUIS MACNEICE (1907–1963) British poet and classical scholar

MAURICE MAETERLINCK (1862–1949) Belgian count, poet, dramatist, and essayist

ANDREW MARVELL (1621–1678) English poet, political writer, and satirist

A. A. MILNE (1882–1956) English poet, playwright, and children's author

PRENTISS MOORE (b. 1947) American poet

WILLIAM MORRIS (1834–1896) English poet and artist

MOTO-ORI NORINAGA (1730–1801) Japanese scholar and poet

ELIZABETH TODD NASH Early-twentieth-century writer

PABLO NERUDA (1904–1973) Chilean poet and diplomat

BEVERLEY NICHOLS (b. 1899) English writer

SAMUEL PARSONS, JR. (1844–1923) American garden writer

ELEANOR PERÉNYI (b. 1918) American garden writer and editor

FERNANDO PESSOA (1888–1935) Portuguese poet; pseudonym Ricardo Reis

SYLVIA PLATH (1932–1963) American poet

PO CHÜ-I (772–846 A.D.) Chinese poet

RICARDO REIS See Fernando Pessoa

RAINER MARIA RILKE (1875–1926) German lyric poet and writer

HANNA RION (b. 1875) American garden writer

JAMES SCHUYLER (1923–1991) American poet and writer

SARA ANDREW SHAFER Early-twentieth-century writer

WILLIAM SHAKESPEARE (1564–1616) English dramatist and poet

LOUISE SHELTON (b. 1867) American garden writer and landscape architect

ALFRED SIMSON Early-twentieth-century writer

CHARLES M. SKINNER Late-nineteenth-century writer

GILBERT SORRENTINO (b. 1929) American poet and novelist

ANNE SPENCER (1882–1975) American poet

EDWARD STEICHEN (1879–1972) American photographer and curator

GERTRUDE STEIN (1874–1946) American writer and feminist

JOHN STEINBECK (1902–1968) American novelist, short-story writer, and social activist

CELIA THAXTER (1835–1894) American poet and garden writer

ROSE FAY THOMAS (1852–1929) American writer

ALICE B. TOKLAS (1877–1967) American feminist

IVAN TURGENEV (1818–1883) Russian novelist

MONA VAN DUYN (b. 1921) American poet

WAKAYAMA KISHI-KO (b. 1888) Japanese poet

CHARLES DUDLEY WARNER (1829–1900) American editor and writer

H. G. WELLS (1866–1946) English novelist, sociological writer, and historian

EDITH WHARTON (1862–1937) American novelist

CANDACE THURBER WHEELER (1827–1923) American writer and fabric and tapestry designer

KATHARINE S. WHITE (1892–1977) American editor and garden writer

WILLIAM CARLOS WILLIAMS (1883–1963) American physician, poet, essayist, and novelist

MISS HENRIETTA WILSON (d. 1862) Scottish garden writer

VIRGINIA WOOLF (1882–1941) English novelist, essayist, and diarist

WILLIAM WORDSWORTH (1770–1850) English poet

MABEL OSGOOD WRIGHT (1859–1934) American nature writer and novelist

RICHARDSON WRIGHT (1887–1961) American editor, journalist, literary critic, and garden writer

PHOTOGRAPHERS

PING AMRANAND was born in Bangkok, Thailand and was educated in England. In addition to *Gardens: An Engagement Calendar for 1991* (Stewart, Tabori & Chang), his book credits include *Untrampled Ground* (Veridion Press) and several travel books. His photographs also appear in *Seven Days in the Kingdom* (Times Editions) and *A Voyage through the Archipelago* (Millet Weldon Owen Publishers). He works regularly for *Southern Accents* and *Historic Preservation,* and his photographs have been featured in *HG, Smithsonian, The Washington Post Sunday Magazine, Architectural Digest,* and *Horticulture.* He divides his time between Bangkok and Kensington, Maryland.

KEN DRUSE has been a contributing garden editor to *House Beautiful* for over a decade, and has written and photographed for periodicals such as *Vogue, HG, Family Circle, Decorating/Remodeling, Horticulture,* and *The New York Times Magazine.* His photographs have appeared in a number of books, and he is both the writer and photographer of *The Natural Garden* (Clarkson Potter), which won awards for Excellence in Writing and Photography from the Garden Writers Association of America, and *The Natural Shade Garden* (Clarkson Potter). He lives in Brooklyn, New York.

RICHARD FELBER is a self-taught photographer whose images of landscapes, gardens, and interiors have appeared in *House Beautiful, HG,* and *Countryside,* as well as in corporate publications. He is the photographer of a book by Mary Jenkins on public gardens in America (Stewart, Tabori & Chang), and a book on herbs (William Morrow). He lives in South Kent, Connecticut.

MICK HALES was born in Worthing, England and grew up in England, Pakistan, and Nigeria. Among his books are *Perfect Preserves* (Stewart, Tabori & Chang) and *Myrtle Allen's Cooking at Ballymaloe House* (Stewart, Tabori & Chang). His photographs have appeared in such magazines as *HG, Connoisseur,* and *Elle Decor.* He lives in Cold Spring, New York.

HARRY HARALAMBOU is a Greek, Cypriot-born photographer who has been photographing gardens throughout the world for the past ten years. His editorial credits include *European Travel & Life, Ladies' Home Journal, Architectural Digest, Town & Country,* and *The New York Times.* His photographs have been featured in seven books on horticulture, including *Specialty Gardens* (Stewart, Tabori & Chang). He lives and gardens in Peconic, New York.

PETER C. JONES is the author of *The Changing Face of America* (Simon & Schuster) and the photographer of *Social Gardens* (Stewart, Tabori & Chang). His photographs are included in the permanent collections of the Museum of Modern Art and the Metropolitan Museum of Art, and his articles and photographs have appeared in *Connoisseur, New England Monthly,* and *HG.* He has organized numerous photography exhibitions throughout the United States and Europe, and serves as a consultant to the Philadelphia Museum of Art. He lives in Manhattan with his wife Charlotte Frieze, the author of *Social Gardens.*

PETER MARGONELLI decided to study photography after seeing a Man Ray retrospective in New York during the mid-1970s, and his interest in landscape photography developed during several years of travel in Europe, the Middle East, and India. His photographs have been published in such periodicals as *HG, House Beautiful,* and *Countryside,* and he is the photographer for a book by Margaret Parke on cutting gardens (Stewart, Tabori & Chang). He lives in Manhattan.

HUGH PALMER is the photographer of *Gardens: An Engagement Calendar for 1992* (Stewart, Tabori & Chang) and his photographs have appeared in periodicals including *Town & Country, HG,* and *Country Life.* Among the fourteen books to his credit are *Private Gardens of England* (Weidenfeld & Nicolson), *The Gardens of Oxford and Cambridge* (Macmillan), and *Garden Ornament* (Thames & Hudson). He lives in a small village in Oxfordshire, England with his wife and two children.

CURTICE TAYLOR is the photographer of *Gardens: An Engagement Calendar for 1990* (Stewart, Tabori & Chang) and a book by Patrick Taylor on the gardens of Belgium and Holland (Stewart, Tabori & Chang). His photographs have been published in *HG, Garden Design, Vogue, House Beautiful,* and *Country Life,* among other magazines. Shown by a number of art galleries, his work is included in numerous corporate and private collections. He is a photography department faculty member at the School of Visual Arts in New York City and lives in Manhattan.

Every effort was made to ensure the accuracy of the sources cited and grateful acknowledgment is made to those who granted permission to reprint the following:

PAGE 5: "This is the garden: colours come and go" from *Collected Poems 1913–1962* by e. e. cummings. Published by MacGibbon & Kee, an imprint of HarperCollins Publishers Ltd. Reprinted by permission of Harper-Collins Publishers Ltd. and Liveright Publishing Corporation.

PAGE 12: "Poem" reprinted from *The Garden in Winter and Other Poems* by Prentiss Moore. Copyright © 1981 by permission of the author and the University of Texas Press.

PAGE 18: From *Down the Garden Path* by Beverley Nichols. Copyright © 1932 by Doubleday, a division of Bantam Doubleday Dell Publishing Group, Inc. Used by permission of Doubleday, a division of Bantam Doubleday Dell Publishing Group, Inc.

PAGE 21: "The Primrose" from *The Complete Poetry of John Donne,* copyright © 1967 by Doubleday & Company, Inc.

PAGE 23: "Diary Entry of 1870" from *The Note-books and Papers of Gerard Manley Hopkins.* Copyright © 1959 by The Society of Jesus. Oxford University Press, 1959.

PAGES 24–27: Extract taken from *The Secret Garden* by Frances Hodgson Burnett, published by Puffin Books.

PAGE 28: "To Make Syrop of Violets" from *The Good House Wife's Jewell,* 1585.

PAGE 29: "Cherry Blossoms" by Moto-ori Norinaga, from *Masterpieces of Japanese Poetry Ancient and Modern* translated and annotated by Miyamori Asatarō. Greenwood Press, 1970.

PAGE 30: "Sonnet 5" and "Letter of June, 1914" from *Sonnets to Orpheus* by Rainer Maria Rilke, translated by M. D. Herter Norton. Copyright © 1942 by W. W. Norton & Company, Inc.

PAGE 33: "Flowers and Insects" from *Nature in a City Yard* by Charles M. Skinner. The Century Company, 1897.

PAGE 34: "The Daffodil and Narcissus" from *The Garden of Pleasant Flowers,* 1629. "Daffodowndilly" from *When We Were Very Young* by A. A. Milne. Copyright © 1924 by E.P. Dutton, renewed 1952 by A. A. Milne.

Used by permission of Dutton Children's Books, a division of Penguin Books USA Inc., and by permission of Methuen Children's Books.

PAGE 36: "Perhaps you'd like to buy a flower" from *The Complete Poems of Emily Dickinson,* edited by Thomas H. Johnson. Little, Brown & Co.

PAGES 38–39: "April" from *In a Gloucestershire Garden* by Henry N. Ellacombe. Edward Arnold, 1896.

PAGE 41: Anonymous poem "Forget-me-not" from *One Hundred and One Legends of Flowers* by Elizabeth Todd Nash. Copyright © 1927 by The Christopher Publishing House.

PAGES 42–44: "Tulips" from *The Collected Poems of Sylvia Plath,* edited by Ted Hughes. Copyright © 1962 by Ted Hughes. Reprinted by permission of HarperCollins Publishers.

PAGE 45: "Peas of the Seedy Buds of Tulips" by Sir Kenelm Digby from *Flower Chronicles* by Buckner Hollingsworth. Rutgers University Press, 1958.

PAGE 46: "Flowers of 'Our Lady'" from *One Hundred and One Legends of Flowers* by Elizabeth Todd Nash. Copyright © 1927 by . The Christopher Publishing House.

PAGES 48–51: "Lilacs" from *The Complete Poetical Works of Amy Lowell.* Copyright © 1955 by Houghton Mifflin Company. Copyright renewed © 1983 by Houghton Mifflin Company, Brinton P. Roberts, and G. D'Andelot Belin, Esquire. Reprinted by permission of Houghton Mifflin Company. All rights reserved.

PAGES 52–53: "Cheddar Pinks" from *Poetical Works of Robert Bridges.* Oxford University Press, 1936.

PAGE 55: "The Franklin's Tale" from *The Canterbury Tales* by Geoffrey Chaucer. Selected version and translation from *Chaucer for Children: A Golden Key* by Mrs. H. R. Haweis. Chatto & Windus, 1877.

PAGE 56: "Dandelions" from *The Collected Poems of Louis MacNeice.* Copyright © 1966 by the estate of Louis MacNeice. Used by permission of Faber & Faber Ltd.

PAGES 58–61: "The Ways of Wistaria" from *Flowers and Fruit* by Colette. Translation copyright © 1986 by Farrar, Straus & Giroux, Inc. Reprinted by permission of Farrar, Straus & Giroux, Inc.

PAGE 62: "I prefer roses to my country" from *Selected Poems* by Fernando Pessoa, edited and translated by Peter Rickard. Reprinted by permission of University of Edinburgh Press.

PAGE 63: "The Magnolia" from *Vegetation* by Francis Ponge, translated by Lee Fahnestock. Red Dust, 1962. Copyright © 1971 by Editions Gallimard. Used by permission of Lee Fahnestock and Editions Gallimard.

PAGE 65: *Let's Make a Flower Garden* by Hanna Rion. Copyright © 1912 by McBride, Nast & Co.

PAGE 66: Excerpt from *The Language of Flowers.* Osborn & Buckingham, 1834.

PAGES 67–68: "The Little Garden and the Peony" from *Peonies in the Little Garden* by Mrs. Edward Harding. Atlantic Monthly Press, 1923.

PAGES 70–71: "What Ails My Fern?" from *A Few Days* by James Schuyler. Copyright © 1984 by James Schuyler.

PAGE 74: Excerpt from *An Island Garden* by Celia Thaxter. Copyright © 1894 by Houghton Mifflin Company.

PAGE 77: Excerpt from *Content in a Garden* by Candace Wheeler. Houghton Mifflin Company and The Riverside Press, 1901.

PAGE 79: "Painting the Landscape" from *Our Mountain Garden* by Rose Fay Thomas. Copyright © 1904 by The Macmillan Company; second edition copyright © 1915 by E. P. Dutton & Company.

PAGES 80–81: "The Tuft of Flowers" from *Robert Frost Poetry and Prose* edited by Edward Connery Lathem. Reprinted by permission of Random Century Group and Jonathan Cape Ltd.

INDEX OF AUTHORS

INDEX OF PHOTOGRAPHERS

INDEX OF TITLES

INDEX OF SUBJECTS

Numbers in **boldface** type indicate illustrations.

Designed by Julie Rauer

Composed in Berkeley Book, Trajan Bold,
and Charlemagne by
Pearl Pressman Liberty Communications Group,
Philadelphia, Pennsylvania

Printed and bound by
Toppan Printing Company, Ltd.,
Tokyo, Japan